Toyg...

The Insider's Guide to Sex Toys & Techniques

Sadie Allison

Illustrated by Steve Lee

ticklekitty®
press

San Francisco

Author: Sadie Allison
Editor-In-Chief: Rich Lippman
Creative Director: Richard G. Martinez
Editor: Joe Azar
Graphic Design: Art Thug Studios (artthug.com)
Research Assistant: John McCoy

Illustrator: Steve Lee
Logo Design: Todd La Rose
Cover Photo: Cliff Lipson
Author Photo: Tony Metaxas
Foreplay Photo: Richard G. Martinez

Published by Tickle Kitty Press
3701 Sacramento Street #107
San Francisco, CA 94118
United States
Fax: 1-(415) 876-1900
http://www.ticklekitty.com

Please Note
This book is intended for educational and entertainment purposes only. Neither the Author,
Illustrator, nor Publisher is responsible for the use or misuse of any sexual aids or techniques
discussed here, or for any loss, damage, injury or ailment caused by reliance on any
information contained in this book. Please use common sense. If you have any health issues
or other concerns, you should consult a qualified medical professional or licensed therapist
BEFORE trying any device or technique. Please read and carefully follow all instructions that
come with any sexual aids you decide to use. The mention of any product or service in this
book does not constitute an endorsement.

10   9   8

Table of contents

f Fore play

I know something about you. You're a lover of excitement, sexual adventure and mind-blowing orgasms—or you want to be. So c'mon in, I've got some heart-pounding ideas for you.

Every human being is wired for pleasure. The key is knowing how to throw the switch—not just a little, but wide open. That's what my book is about. Safe, private, life-affirming, sheet-grabbing, scream-out-loud, scrape-me-off-the ceiling orgasms. And thanks to the miracles of machines, electricity and inventors with wild imaginations, there's a world of toys out there waiting for you—whether you're solo, monogamous, or hot 'n heavy with a new lover.

Sure there's a ton of choices. But no need to be confused or intimidated—help is here!

Sex toys are designed exclusively for pleasure, but must also be used with respect for safety, hygiene and comfort. This is true whether you use them by yourself—or with your partner. I'll guide you through it all, whether you're a bit shy, a sexual connoisseur, or somewhere in between. I've tried many of these toys myself, so you'll read my first-hand experiences, as well as tips from other women and men who have confided in me. Look for my 'Sadie Sez' advice throughout the book.

You'll find out the easiest way to introduce your lover to a sex toy for the first time. You'll explore the colorful world of buzzing, vibrating, pulsating orgasm-givers. You'll discover new pleasure tricks that maximize ecstasy for you—as well as your lover. And you'll feel totally reassured that there's nothing wrong or unusual about receiving pleasure like this—you've just graduated to adult toys.

Ladies, no matter where you are on the orgasm spectrum, this fun's for you. If you have yet to orgasm—this guide will help you get there (along with a very big smile!). If you enjoy orgasms—but all too infrequently—I'll help you experience bigger, better, longer, stronger multiples! And if you're the adventurous type looking for new ways to play, I'm going to give you new heart-pumping ideas to stimulate your creativity and ingenuity!

And guys…if you've never played with sex toys, or think they're only for women— you're in for a big surprise. You may even decide to pass up Monday Night Football for them! And you'll quickly discover that once you give multiple *toygasms* to your woman, she'll constantly beg you for more sex. Can you handle it, big guy??

So what are you waiting for? Dive in. And start enjoying all the *toygasmic* pleasure coming your way. ♥

X's and O's,

Sadie

Sadie

Toygasms!

1

How To Spring A Sex Toy
On Your Lover

Great sex starts with open communication. So if you're eager to introduce a sex toy or two, don't startle your lover by pulling a giant, buzzing phallus out of the nightstand. Spend a few minutes beforehand discussing this new opportunity for adventure. Whether your lover is gung-ho or a bit shy, it's important to consider their feelings and not apply undue pressure if they hesitate. In fact, airing anxieties is often the best way to relax, and both of you could soon be in for a future full of record-breaking orgasms.

Why are people hesitant to try sex toys? Fear and lack of education. Even if they are mildly curious—or fantasize secretly about them—the reality may be a bit overwhelming. Here's the key to introducing a plaything into your repertoire: be patient. You'll discover that a little knowledge about sex toys will help ease your fears and open new doors to sexual exploration with your partner.

Fear, guilt and shame can be rooted in family conditioning, societal pressures or religious upbringing. However, they're no match for the libido, which usually gets its way. After all, discovery and pleasure are healthy, both in life and in bed.

Why Sex Toys Can Increase Sexual Intimacy In Women

Women who resist toyplay the most are also among those who could benefit from it the most. By starting off with a simple toy, either solo or with your lover, you could begin enjoying many more of the physical pleasures you have coming to you, especially if:

♥ You have not yet learned to orgasm, or don't orgasm very often

♥ You're able to orgasm during solo play, but never with your partner

- ♥ You want exciting new pleasures that complement your relationship
- ♥ You want to break out of a sexual rut and rekindle your physical fires
- ♥ You still want pleasure when your man is out of town!

Many thousands of women have enjoyed their first orgasms with the help of a little vibration to send them over the edge. Others have learned to orgasm more easily—either solo or with lovers—and at the same time, increase sexual intimacy. You'll know these people by the sudden appearance of smiles on their faces.

You can then take it to the next level and give your lover one of the most craved treats of all time: let him watch you play with your toy. Don't believe me? Try it when you're ready, and you'll see his eyes widen with awe. There's just something a little naughty about it, and that's okay—it's just the two of you exploring and having fun. Note how special you feel. It's truly empowering, and he'll adore you even more for it.

You may be surprised to learn that many sex therapists and sexuality experts actually prescribe sex toys for their patients. Toys are safe, fun and liberating, once you find the right one (or ones!) for you. And they can be purchased discreetly on the Internet or by catalog, and shipped to you in a plain unmarked box.

Read on. Understanding more about yourself, your comfort, and the modern toys available to you today are your first steps toward enjoying greater sexual intimacy and physical pleasure tomorrow—and for the rest of your life.

Hey Guys: Sex Toys Can Turn You Into A Sex Star!

I know you guys can get just as antsy about introducing sex toys. But once you overcome your hesitation, you may soon discover intimate pleasures you've only dreamed about. And toys offer many other benefits, too:

♥ *You increase your sexual mastery.* If you want to be a bigger star in bed, a toy can help you raise the volume of your partner's orgasms, making her climax easier, more often, and with much greater intensity.

♥ *You add variety to your lovemaking.* Toys give you a new means to satisfy your partner. They're not competition for your hands, penis and tongue, they simply give you a new way to pleasure your partner that will drive her wild and make her crave you more often.

♥ *You gain new steam.* Toys let you continue pleasing your lover after you've been totally satisfied—easily, passionately, completely.

❤ *You earn more appreciation and affection.* When you focus on her pleasure, you'll get a lot more in return.

Attitude Is Everything

You are a great lover. If that's anything but total truth, toys will help—not hurt—your sexual confidence. Do any of these fears sound familiar?

I must not be good enough for her.

Toys are no replacement for you. They don't kiss, whisper sweet nothings, exude pheromones or even take out the garbage. There's no emotional connection. They complement sex, and your lover will usually compliment you. Think of toys as a sexual enhancement designed to bring pleasure to both of you. After all, the more ways you can give your lover orgasms, the more passionate your lover will be with you, and the more you'll be turned on.

Will she still want me as a lover after we start using a toy?

Humans are built for sex; toys are designed for foreplay and fun, or extending the lovemaking after intercourse. So the answer is yes, she will still want you, and now, probably more.

I feel weird about bringing a gadget into bed. Is this normal?

Yes, the sensations and vibrations of another object in bed with you can be a bit unusual the first time, but this doesn't mean there's anything amiss. What could be amiss is that you didn't discuss your desire to bring a toy into bed before the lovemaking began. A gentle conversation about the subject, perhaps eased with a glass of wine and the glow of candlelight can actually inspire the desire you were seeking.

Jack, 36, a high-tech sales exec, wanted to try a vibrator with his girlfriend Janet. "I sat her down and told her I had an important question. 'I really enjoy our sex life,' I said, 'but don't freak out...I'm kinda curious about trying out a sex toy together. I think we'd both enjoy it.'"

"Well, that got Janet's interest right away, and she said she'd be open to exploring it with me. Phew! I thanked her, and suggested we look through a catalog or boutique together to get something she'd really like. She was thrilled—and it all came down to open, honest communication."

How To Bring It Up

Introducing the subject comes naturally to some, while it's awkward for others. Yet, the rewards of acceptance far outweigh any risk you'll take. Here are some suggestions to overcome your fears that have worked for others, and will make those first steps easier on you.

Women: slow and go

When a guy's hot and turned on, he'll go for almost anything, right? Can you think of a better time to bring up that cool little vibrator you discovered?

Start by whispering there's something you found that you REALLY like—then bring out a small, non-phallic vibrator (even if it's not your first choice). Virtually every guy loves watching a woman use a toy on herself, so why not start there? After a little while, you can try it on him—up and down his penis and all around his scrotum. You won't hear any complaints.

Now that you've broken the ice, you can break out even more toys. If you enjoy penetration, start with something smaller than his penis—no guy wants to see a toy that's bigger than him (at first). Give him a sense of control, engage in sexy talk about what you'd like—and find out what would turn him on. Chances are, he'll act like a kid in a candy store.

Guys: work it in

If you have difficulty bringing up this subject, as most guys do, here are some suggestions to make it easier on you:

♥ *Explore this book with your lover.* This will save you the stress of finding the right words to educate her on the pleasures of toys. You'll both find a wealth of common sense advice designed to ease fears and spark passion.

♥ *Be sensual.* Even without any toys, start exploring her in new and erotic ways. Let her feel special by touching her in new places. Use the magic of your hands and fingers. Try delicate strokes and back massages with sensual massage oils. Move the sexual and sensual part of your relationship into a new phase of exploration, so that graduating to sex toys will be part of the natural progression.

♥ *Use humor.* Yep, try bringing up the subject in a funny way. For instance, on your next grocery shopping list, write 'milk, cereal, bread, Love Egg, juice.' Voila, the topic is opened for discussion. Use your imagination—well-timed humor can instantly knock down barriers and lead to open, honest communication.

♥ *Have a look together.* Go online and see an array of

pictures and descriptions of the various toys your lover might like. Or visit a sex toy shop together. After the giggling stops, you may find the toy that's right for both of you. Then be a sport—spring for the purchase and the treat will be all yours!

❤ *Don't push it.* Start with something simple, non-phallic and non-vibrating, like a flavored lube or topical enhancement gel. After that, you can introduce a vibrating egg—small, effective, cute. Make sure she knows that if she says stop, you will stop.

❤ *Reinforce positively.* If she's shy, just leave the vibrating egg with her. She may get curious and try it out on her own. Don't forget to include the batteries! She may surprise you. ❤

Sadie Sez:

Guys! Don't fight 'em, join 'em! Team up with vibrators and win every time!

Toygasms!

Your Next Stop:
The Erogenous Zone

Erogenous Zones: *areas of the human body that can be sexually arousing when touched and caressed, either by your partner or by yourself.*

Do you know your most powerful sex organ? Look up. It's your brain. It's where your body receives its most powerful sexual signals, such as attitudes, desires and fantasies. In short, your turn-ons—and your turn-offs. Often gaining a better understanding about your body can turn off a hang-up forever—leaving you freer to explore and enjoy your own sexuality.

Female Anatomy 101

The female body is one of nature's most beautiful works of art. Soft, curvy, sensual, erotic. Regrettably, many women aren't really acquainted with their very own masterpiece. Yet simply by becoming comfortable with your own touch-sensitive areas— and understanding a little more about them—you'll quickly enhance your own pleasure, sensually and sexually.

 Sadie Sez:

A small hand mirror can help, too!

Vulva. The external genitals—the labia minora and labia majora (inner and outer skin folds or "lips"), the tip of the clitoris ("clit"), the prepuce (clitoral foreskin or "hood"), two Bartholin's glands (which produce lubrication during arousal) and the urethral and vaginal openings.

Labia majora and labia minora. The lips of soft skin on the vulva's outermost parts (labia majora) designed to protect the inner folds (labia minora) and inner vulva. Both sets of lips, especially the labia minora, are highly pleasurable erogenous zones that swell with blood while reacting to touch and penetration.

Clitoris. This is a woman's orgasm nerve center—the primary source of sexual pleasure. The tip of the clitoris is located at the top of the vulva, hidden slightly under the clitoral hood, where the inner and outer labia meet. You can see it by gently parting the labia. It's about the

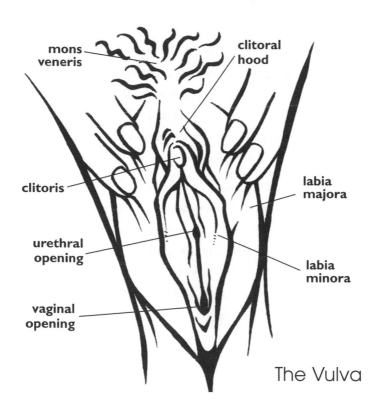

mons veneris

clitoral hood

clitoris

labia majora

urethral opening

labia minora

vaginal opening

The Vulva

size of a pea. The two clitoral shafts (crura or "legs") extend inward and straddle each side of the vaginal canal.

Vagina. In its unexcited state, this canal usually measures three to four inches deep, but can actually double in depth and width when aroused. Of course, it's designed by nature to be elastic, since it must also stretch to accommodate a newborn.

G-spot. Located inside the vagina, near the roof, about three-quarters of the way up, this small spongy area is a highly pleasurable erogenous zone. The G-spot, also known as a urethral sponge because it surrounds and protects the urethra, responds pleasurably to stroking and pressure in many women.

Pelvic muscles. You know these muscles, because they're what you use to control urination. Both women and men have the PC (pubococcygeus) muscles. During arousal and climax, the PC muscles contract involuntarily— randomly at first, then building into rhythmic, pleasurable contractions during orgasm. Women can actually increase vaginal tightness and orgasmic intensity with Kegel exercises—just squeeze and release these muscles.

Mons veneris. Latin for "Hill of Venus" (the Roman goddess of love), the mons veneris is the soft cushiony area that sits on your pubic bone. The hair protects this area of your body, while the mons protects the pubic bone from impact during intercourse.

 Sadie Sez:

Make Kegels part of your daily routine. Flex your pelvic muscles at your desk, in your car, doing your hair, watching TV! No one will know but you.

Breasts, areolas and nipples. A sensual erogenous zone, your breasts, nipples and areolas (small rings of color around each nipple) can be sources of great pleasure. Stimulation can make the nipples erect and sensitive to touch during your pleasure sessions. Some women experience orgasm from nipple stimulation alone!

Anus, rectum and sphincter. Full of densely concentrated nerve endings, this erogenous zone can be quite sensitive to touch. Stimulating these nerve endings can be intensely pleasurable, even orgasmic.

Perineum. This is the small area between the bottom of the vulva and the anus. Many find gentle teasing and stroking of this area to be extremely pleasurable.

Male Anatomy 101

Because a male's genitals are external—and deliver pure primal 'motivation' all day long—guys tend to be self-proclaimed experts on their own sexual anatomy. Let's just see how much you guys *really* know:

♥ *Shaft.* It's made up of two sections of spongy erectile tissue and blood vessels, plus a third section that extends to the tip of the penis. To create an erection, these tissues fill with blood.

♥ *Glans.* The most sensitive part of the penis, the glans ("head") contains the greatest number of nerve endings, making it very similar to the clitoris in women. At the bottom edge of the glans is the frenulum, which connects the glans to the shaft, and has many nerve endings which produce pleasure for men during stroking.

♥ *Testicles.* This is where testosterone and sperm are produced. Located inside the scrotum ("sack"), these two organs are best handled delicately, though some men find gentle stretching or tugging to be pleasurable.

♥ *Prostate.* This is the organ that produces the ejaculatory fluid, which later mixes with sperm to make semen. It is located below the bladder and behind the pubic bone, and can be stimulated through the anus. A pleasure center in men, many can climax from direct prostate stimulation.

💜 *Anus.* The anus has a high concentration of nerve endings and can evoke significant pleasure for men. While some men consider anal stimulation to be unnatural or only okay for women, others discover it can provide many new sensations and orgasms.

💜 *Perenium.* Extending from the back of the scrotum to the front of the anus, the perineum is often overlooked as an erogenous zone that merits exploration. Also known as the 'taint.'

💜 *Nipples.* A man's nipples can be every bit as sensitive as a woman's, and many men enjoy gentle sucking, stroking or pinching from their partners. 💜

2

Toygasms!

∽ᗒ♡ᗕ∾

3 Getting Ready For Pleasure

Whether you're planning for a solitary experience—or one shared with a partner—a few simple steps can help you get comfortable to free your mind and body.

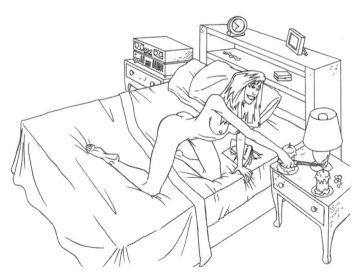

Toygasms!

♥ *Set the stage.* Disconnect your phone, cellular or pager. Accent your surroundings to create just the right ambiance. And be sure to gather any visual and sexual aids on your romantic menu within arm's reach.

♥ *Sound.* Select the music to match your mood: slow and romantic for sexy and sensual; upbeat for pump-it-up action. Flip in a long-playing CD so you won't be interrupted by mood-busting commercials on the radio.

♥ *Candles and lighting.* Nothing beats a soft glow for romantic ambiance. Light the candles—and dim the lights.

♥ *Temperature.* Warmer air may ignite your passions, but cooler air might increase your sensitivity. Choose accordingly.

♥ *Aroma.* Scented candles, perfumes, flowers or incense can provide intimate, subtle aromas to heighten the senses. Just don't overdo it.

♥ *Location location location.* Don't limit yourself to the bed or couch—playing in the bathtub or shower adds spice!

♥ *Entertainment.* Videos, magazines, erotic literature or Internet sites can all accompany toy play with great visuals for titillation or fantasy.

♥ *Privacy.* For heaven's sake, put the kids to bed…and make sure they're asleep! Don't let an innocent request for 'a glass of water' mess up your well-deserved orgasm.

♥ *Talk it up.* Don't be shy to whisper sweet dirty nothings to your partner!

The Clitoral Waltz

The clitoris is the nerve center for orgasm—and is your primary source of sexual pleasure. Many women are unable to reach orgasm through intercourse alone, and require some form of clitoral stimulation to achieve climax.

The clitoris' head is located at the top of the vulva, hidden slightly under the hood, where the inner and outer labia meet. About the size of a pea, the clitoris can be viewed by gently parting the labia. The clitoris can also be compared to a penis, though it's obviously smaller in size. Like a penis, the clitoris has erectile tissue and a very high concentration of nerve endings. This highly sensitive organ swells with blood when sexually aroused, becoming erect and possibly doubling in size. Bringing the clitoris to this erect state during sex-toy play helps lead up to orgasm. Its sensitivity to touch varies greatly among women.

Using your fingers or toys to stimulate the clitoris is a fundamental skill for arousal. It's important to get familiar with your clitoris and learn the stroking styles that work best for you. As you develop this skill, concentrate on increasing your state of arousal and observe the sensations your clitoris produces. With proper stimulation, the clitoris' small head, underneath the clitoral hood, will swell with blood and begin to appear. The more aroused you get, the more erect and visible the head becomes. Once the clitoris is clearly erect and visible, you're on your way to orgasm.

Whether you prefer tortuous finesse, or rapid massage—or both—using the right motions at the right moment will trigger the most intense orgasms of your life. Try these just with your hand. Then use a dildo or vibrator for added ecstacy.

Clitoris Cuddle
Place two fingers side by side over the top of your clitoris. Apply just enough pressure while rubbing in circular motions. Try varying the speed and pressure with small to large circles. You'll know when you're in the rhythm—you may orgasm very quickly.

Three-Finger Rub
Place your index finger and your ring finger on the top inside areas of your outer labia. Spread

the labia out against your body, holding your lips apart. Now your middle finger is in perfect position to stimulate your fully exposed clitoris, and your other hand is free for sex-toy play!

Figure Eights

Glide one or more fingers up, over and around your clitoral area in figure eights. Use small figures, focusing on the tip of your clitoris, or larger figures, stimulating the entire clitoris and inner labia. You can also start at the top of the vulva, near the clitoris, and guide your fingers down to the bottom near your vaginal opening at the lower part of the "eight." Now get creative and rub your way from one to ten!

Side Winder

Place one fingertip on each side of your clitoris. Slide your fingers vertically, up and down, up and down, stimulating your sensitive inner labia as well as your clitoris.

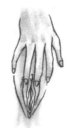

Hand Job

For fuller stimulation, snuggly position three or four of your fingers, side by side and flat, between your outer labia. Apply

pressure and stroke yourself with the motion that gives you the most pleasure.

Tap Tap Tap

With one hand, gently separate your outer labia, fully exposing your clitoris. With the index finger on your other hand, lightly tap your clitoris, changing the speed and pressure to your own delight.

Finger Roll

Place your thumb and middle finger around your clitoris, then gently squeeze and lift. Now roll it delicately between your fingers. Start softly, slowly, gradually picking up the pace and pressure. Try light pinches and tugs. Like it? Do more!

What If You're Pregnant?

You don't have to give up your sexual pleasures. Just observe a few simple lovemaking rules to ensure the safety of you and your baby. Start by asking your physician. Don't be embarrassed— you wouldn't be there in the first place if not for sex!

Intercourse, as well as dildos and insertable vibrators, are generally safe during low-risk pregnancies as long as you're

Sadie Sez:

Recover from pregnancy quicker. Perform daily Kegel exercises to tighten up the pelvic floor muscles to get you back into multiple orgasmic shape!

careful not to harm the opening of the cervix at the back of the vaginal canal. Use plenty of lubricant (see next chapter), and make sure your toys are ultra-clean. You're okay to climax, too— as often as you like! It's a myth that this will induce premature labor. Orgasms during pregnancy can help calm cramping and bloating, relieve headaches and help you sleep better.

If you're more comfortable without penetration, there's a wealth of vibrators today for you to use topically. Choose the one that will accommodate any new sensitivities you're feeling during pregnancy. If your desire for sex has declined during this time, a vibrator may be just the ticket for you and your lover. ♥

3

Toygasms!

4 Lubricants Of Love

I f you've never tried sexual lubricants ("lube"), or haven't used the slippery stuff in a while, you're in for a treat. Lubricants help you enhance your sexual ecstasy without any risk—and they cost next to nothing.

Whether you're self-pleasuring, using a toy, or engaging in passionate intercourse, lubrication increases your sensitivity by creating smoother, slipperier surfaces wherever you choose to apply it. Slathered on sex toys, they become safer and easier to use. On your lover, you'll discover a new level of ecstasy. And on your own erogenous zones, you'll find yourself on the ceiling!

Sex lubricants come in two main varieties: water- or silicone-based. Here are the advantages of each:

Water-Based Lubes

Similar to the feel of natural vaginal fluids, you can find water-based lubes in a variety of consistencies, from liquid to jelly. Liquid varieties are ideal for all-around play, while jellies tend to have more lasting power for extended encounters. However, they may not last long enough for anal pleasure. Water-based lubes are ideal to use with condoms. There are also flavored varieties for use during oral sex. Water-based lubes rarely irritate, and wash easily out of sheets, bedspreads and auto upholstery! Toy clean-up is easy, too. And as for you, it's an easy wash-off with a wet wash cloth.

Silicone-Based Lubes

A super-slippery lube, silicone lasts and lasts for longer friction-free fun. This makes it ideal for in-the-water sex or anal play. It's also compatible with safer-sex practices, such as condoms or latex gloves. Because it doesn't break down in water, though, your shower or tub surfaces could become slippery. Be sure to use cautiously and clean up thoroughly.

Warning! Never use household products as lubricant! Petroleum jelly, massage oil, hand lotion and cooking oil are awful choices for lube, because they aren't made to go inside your body, can cause infections and will also break down latex condoms.

 Sadie Sez:

You can never use too much lube. The slipperier, the merrier!

Lube On Up—Slide On Down

Here are a few tips to help you get the most out of your friction-free fun.

Variety. Lubes vary widely in viscosity, texture and taste from brand to brand. Lucky for you, many manufacturers offer

Sadie Sez:

A little saliva or a few drops of water can quickly reactivate previously applied lubrication during playtime!

trial sizes and freebies so you can find the lube that works best for you.

Anal pleasure. Lubrication is absolutely necessary during anal play. Unlike the vagina, the anus doesn't produce natural lubrication. So lube it up and slide it in!

Individual sensitivities. Certain lubes contain ingredients that may not agree with you. Glycerin can promote the growth of yeast cultures in women who are prone to infections. Nonoxynol-9 (N-9), can be highly irritating to some women (and its HIV-fighting abilities are now in dispute). Flavoring agents, while fun, can sometimes cause irritation.

Natural massage oils. Some swear by natural food-grade oils found in health food stores. Just be sure to avoid oils that have sugar—they can cause yeast infections.

Toy don'ts. Silicone lube can damage silicone toys. Use water-based lube, or simply apply a condom to your toy. ♥

5 Dildos— Ready When You Are

Dildos: *non-vibrating toys, made in many different shapes and sizes, used for vaginal and anal penetration as well as clitoral stroking.*

How long have dildos been around? 100 years? 200 years? A millennium? Think again, because they've been in use as long as women have had a sex drive. You'll see dildos depicted in ancient art, and history shows they were created and adored by women in many cultures, from Greece to China, India and beyond.

Toygasms!

A dildo (or dong) describes any toy designed to be inserted vaginally or anally. Dildos don't vibrate, so if it takes a battery, it's not a dildo (although some vibrators look phallic and are designed for insertion). Today, they come in a variety of lengths, shapes, diameters and colors—a far cry from the one large Caucasian replica that dominated dildo sales for years. Heck, you can even get a dildo today that glows in the dark!

For solo ecstasy, dildos are fun, simple and safe—offering you the greatest amount of control, for you and only you determine the degree and angle of penetration, thrusting speed and all other creative uses. And with the added pressure and sexual fullness they provide, they're the best for earth-shaking vaginal orgasms. As you'll see later in this book, you can also use one in tandem with a vibrator, creating nearly unlimited possibilities for orgasms.

Dildos open up many exciting options for partner sex, too. And since penetration isn't a dildo's only purpose, you can enjoy intense pleasure when your lover positions it for friction across your clitoris, down between the labia and just inside the vaginal opening. With an added dab of lube, you'll quickly be in *toygasm* heaven!

With so many choices today, you'll find all the advice you need in this chapter to narrow them down to your favorites. You can then leaf through a catalog or visit an online sex shop—or take a field trip to a local sex boutique. Some shops display

Sadie Sez:

Don't forget, the human hand is one of the best sex toys of all time—yours AND your lover's.

samples outside their packages, perfect for an up-close touch-test—so you can choose the toy that's got the texture, heft and flexibility (or stiffness) to fan your flames.

The Dildo Debate: Porous vs. Non-Porous

Porous or non-porous, that is the question. Sex toys made of porous materials (such as latex rubber) can be soft like your skin, but also need to be kept extra clean. If not, bacteria and viruses can live in the tiny openings (pores) on the surface. Porous toys are also known to absorb lube quickly, so you'll have to apply it more frequently.

Sex toys made of non-porous materials (such as silicone or glass) offer smooth surfaces, and have no pores where germs can hide. This makes them easier to keep clean, however you should always clean your toys after each use. A little lube goes a long way with non-porous toys.

Narrowing Your Choices

So many dildos, so little time

Silicone. Among the highest quality dildos, many women love silicone for its lifelike feel and ability to retain body heat. Non-porous and easy to clean (dishwasher safe/top rack!), they can last for years. They're mostly hypoallergenic, too. Just watch out for cracks or cuts that may develop that can harbor germs. And since silicone cannot be repaired, be prepared to retire your ol' buddy if he should ever tear.

Latex. You'll find latex rubber dildos everywhere, but they also have their limitations. Not as lifelike and firm as silicone, they still serve their purpose well. Be sure to clean up thoroughly, as latex is porous and can harbor germs. People who like this material, but have allergic reactions to latex, might find pleasure in jelly or silicone dildos.

Jelly. A popular innovation of the nineties, jellies come in a playful array of bright, semi-translucent colors. Jellies are less expensive than most other dildos, a bit more delicate, and porous—so wash them with adult toy cleanser or warm soapy water after each use.

Lifelike. Soft and fleshy, with a feeling of real human skin, these new-generation materials are a true delight. They require extra care to keep clean because of their porous material, but are well worth having in your treasure collection. Also, store them apart from other toys: when left in direct contact, the composition can degrade.

Acrylic. Do you like your dildos HARD? Then a plastic or acrylic dildo is for you. They're easy to clean because they're non-porous, and enable you to reach your G-spot and anal erogenous zones with an abundance of pressure.

Vinyl. Basic, reliable and affordable, what vinyl lacks in flexibility it makes up in durability. Available in just a few colors, including a little pink version ideal for anal play, it's thankfully non-porous and easy to clean.

Glass. At first thought, glass may seem like an odd choice. But wait till you see what's available today! Glass dildos come in a wide variety of vivid colors and creative shapes—some with exotic liquids inside that glow in the dark. Built to last a lifetime by the craftsmen who make glass pipes, they're similar in hardness to acrylics, and designed for both vaginal and anal pleasure. They're hypo-allergenic, non-porous and dishwasher

safe—and retain warmth and coolness. They're pricier, but worth every penny.

Metal. A rare find today for experienced toy enthusiasts and collectors. Cool to the touch, metal dildos slowly warm up with use. Be extra careful moving around with a metal toy inside you, as you can bruise your tailbone or pelvic bone with any quick, jarring motions.

How Big?

You can find dildos small as a finger, thick as a neck, or as long as an arm! Choosing the right size depends on your own taste, the capacity of your vagina and how you want to use your

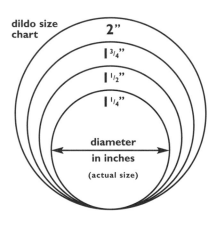

dildo size chart

2"

1 ³/₄"

1 ¹/₂"

1 ¹/₄"

diameter
in inches
(actual size)

dildo. Dildos are measured by thickness (diameter across, not circumference around) and length (base to tip). You can choose a thickness the size of a pencil eraser to over three inches, and a length the size of your pinky to, well, use your imagination!

If you like pressure and fullness inside your vagina, or just clitoral stroking without much thrusting, then four inches long should be ideal. But if you plan to thrust in and out, and stimulate your G-spot, then go for seven or more inches with a flared base or one with testicles for an easy grip.

Sizing Up The Right Dildo For You

Start by looking at what you currently enjoy for penetration, whether it's a finger, penis, carrot or other handy object. If it's satisfying, then that measure is a good place to start. You can always upgrade later to a slightly larger size and enjoy a newly enhanced feeling of fullness. But don't go too wild: a dildo that's too big can be uncomfortable or painful.

Ready to go for it? Consider this:

Material. Do you like soft gentle caressing—or a stiffer, harder ride that reaches your G-spot?

Size/thickness. Start smaller than you think necessary— move up to bigger sizes when you're ready.

Length. How deep do you like it? Are you a 'play-at-the-entrance' type—or 'deep thruster'?

Firmness. If you'll be enjoying G-spot stimulation, or strapping one on, you'll usually want a firmer, longer dildo.

Design. Which floats your boat: realistic, semi-real or smooth? Visit a sex boutique or online retailer for a first-hand look.

Price. Jelly toys are more affordable, latex is in the middle of the range, and glass and silicone are the highest priced—but also the best you can get!

Which Shapes Turn You On?

Face it: there's a dildo for you. That's because there are hundreds of shapes and sizes:

Realistic. Imagine a dildo so lifelike, you'd swear there's a guy attached to it! That's because they're molded from real penises, some of them famous porn stars. They're designed to offer you incredibly lifelike sensations, including vivid veins, bouncing testicles and kissable skin texture.

Semi-real. These dildos are slightly scaled down models—offering many of the lifelike anatomical features as above, but without the extremely detailed folds of skin or veins. They tend to be a bit smoother, and can be found with wild

Nicky, 18, and just beginning to explore her sexuality, had to navigate around her restrictive parents.

"I respect my parents and appreciate that sex is complicated— enough to make a mess out of life if I don't deal with it right. I can see their point that sex will be a bit easier to handle when I'm a little older. But I don't want to wait! I have these really strong sexual urges and I'm tired of using my fingers all the time.

By shopping on the net, I was able to get a basic dildo that I use along with my fingers. What a difference! Now I can imagine what it must feel like to have a guy inside me, and I don't have to worry about my parents or getting pregnant."

designs and non-flesh colors. And with fewer lifelike crevices, they may also be easier to clean.

Smooth. A smooth dildo only abstractly resembles a penis, often with a perfectly smooth shaft and a head that's only slightly lifelike. If you prefer texture and friction against your labia and inside your vagina, a smooth surface might not provide enough excitement, but it can be a good starter for first-timers who want a gentle, super-soothing experience. They're also easy on the eyes.

Toygasms!

Abstract. Not just for artistic expression or playful variety, abstract dildos are often created to get around laws in countries such as Japan, where the manufacture of sex toys that precisely mimic human genitals are outlawed. So take your pick: creative shapes, animals, corn, cucumbers, goddesses, ex-Presidents!

Doubles. Double-penetrators are designed for simultaneous vaginal and anal penetration. They consist of two prongs, the smaller one used anally. Double penetrators also come in vibrating models. Double-enders are extra long shafts (18" or more), made from soft, flexible materials and have a head at

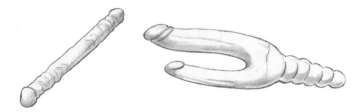

each end. They are popular with lesbian couples, but can also be used during self-loving sessions for twice the pleasure!

Anal. Dildos designed for anal play come in semi-real or smooth finishes, and in many different lengths and sizes, usually with a flared base. Of course, any dildo can be used for anal play—just be sure to wrap it in a fresh condom when switching between the vagina and anus, use lots of lube, and most of all, go slooowwwly! *The Anal Playground* (Chapter 7) has a lot more information on this pleasure zone.

Coming Attractions

Like factory options? Check these out

Suction cups. Attached to the back of your dildo, this feature lets you stick it anywhere you want: floor, wall, toilet seat, bedpost, shower wall, bathtub and table. This gives you added freedom for just about any position, speed, depth and angle of penetration you want. Squat for that deep fullness, or back into it for total satisfaction. Plus, the hands-free operation leaves your fingers to do the walking!

Testicles. Whether you use them to cushion your backward thrusting, as a hand-grip for thrusting, or simply because you enjoy the "slapping balls" effect, there is a variety of balled dildos for you to choose from.

Dingers. Why settle only for what Mother Nature created? If you like a big, round head that's much larger than the glans of a man's penis, this will feel really good during vaginal penetration!

Inflatables. This model comes with a small hand pump that gradually expands the dildo in size and firmness. Try inserting the dildo while soft, then control the expansion of size and pressure to your liking.

Self-Satisfying Dildo Pleasure Tricks

For all the techniques below, simply relax and concentrate on your 'getting into a rhythm' movement. Do what feels good— from clitoral stroking to thrusting—at your own pace and pleasure. Fine-tune your movements by focusing on your own hot spots, and simply let your body take over. Mmmmmm.

"Gettin' To Know You"

The perfect starter technique, you can enjoy it just about anywhere you like: on your back, sitting up with a leg hung over a chair, or even on a plush carpet on the floor. Lube up and gently penetrate your vaginal opening with the head of the toy. Glide in and out with short, slow strokes. Go deeper, go faster, but go at your

own pace! Try rubbing your clitoris with your other hand at the same time. Then experiment with different stroking styles, or next time, pick up a slightly bigger dildo for added pleasure inside.

"Surprise From Behind"

Attach a suction cup dildo to any hard, smooth vertical surface, preferably close to the floor. Lube it thoroughly. Place pillows under your knees, and ease yourself back. Notice you have complete control of speed and thrusting. If your dildo has testicles, you'll have the added bonus of a "cushion" to pump against. Now try staying still for a moment to experience the feeling of "fullness" while you stroke your clitoris with your fingers or a vibrator. You may be surprised to see how deep you can really penetrate!

"Twist 'n Shout"

This technique simulates the way partners gyrate their hips during intercourse. Hold the base of the dildo, twisting your wrist all the way to the left. Place the toy at the tip of your vaginal opening, now twist it slowly to the right as you penetrate yourself. Continue this twisting and penetrating at a pace that brings you the most pleasure.

Simultaneously, put your fingers from your other hand to work stroking your outer labia. You'll find this easier if you're using a long dildo, or one with a testicle-grip.

"Petunia Slide"

Start with a textured dildo—one that's fairly flexible, perhaps with veins or bumps molded into the shaft. After you've teased yourself with your fingers, slowly slide the tip of the dildo into your vaginal opening—just far enough so the tip stays in place while you bend the shaft upwards toward your clitoris.

Now start sliding the dildo deeper into your vagina, so the texture stays in constant contact with your clitoris and inner vulva. You may want to keep one hand down at the vaginal opening, so the tip doesn't slip out as you guide it back and forth. Vulva-riffic!

"Wild 'n Slippery Suction Slide"

Here are the ingredients for this wet, wild, orgasmic ride: suction cup dildo, water-based lube, shower stall, plenty of hot water.

Step into the shower with the lube and start your juices flowing with your favorite clitoral stroking styles. When you're ready for penetration, pick up the dildo and turn so your back is towards the shower wall. Bend your knees slightly. Hold the dildo parallel with the floor, and right behind your vagina, estimating where to suction the dildo to the wall. Once you find a perfect spot, attach it. Now put plenty of lube on your toy and your vagina.

Slowly begin working it inside you by backing into it as if a lover was behind you. Enjoy the hot, sensual water flowing down your body, embracing you like a phantom lover. Keep working the dildo in, swaying back and forth. Grab onto any handles and use them to push and pull yourself forward and back. (Careful: the doors may not be designed to support the commotion!) Get a good rhythm going, and take it to the limit. Doesn't this feel good?!!

Move your hand down, and begin rubbing your clitoris again. Or use your favorite water proof vibrator. Did that orgasmic moaning come out of YOU?

Sadie Sez:

CAUTION: While silicone lube is usually best for waterplay, it is not recommended here because it could make your shower too slippery. **ALWAYS** proceed with caution when using lube while standing and playing in water.

Toygasms!

"Cowgirl"

On your bed, couch or in front of the fireplace, straddle a pillow, sofa cushion or other soft object between your legs. Place the base of the dildo against the cushion, lube it up and gently slide the dildo up inside yourself. Slide down deeper, and as you get used to this position, let the pillow or cushion absorb some of the energy of your downward thrusts.

Remember: you can gyrate your hips for more stimulation. This technique is also great to use with a G-spot penetrating hands-free vibrator, as discussed in *Vibrators—Get Your Buzz On!* (Chapter 6).

"Poppin' Punani"

If you've never tried a "dinger"—a dildo with a big round head—you're missing out on some enthralling vaginal teasing. While pumping slowly and gently, pull the dinger all the way out with each stroke. Each time you re-enter and exit, you get that sort of "popping," eye-opening, joyous feeling. Continue on with short strokes, exiting and re-entering, or try deeper, longer strokes. You'll find that the oversized head is also ideal for rubbing on your clitoris—which also can cover and stimulate the entire inner vulva at the same time.

Dildoing With Your Partner

There's one sex toy technique that works better than all others: communication. Verbal feedback is the key that tells you if your partner's enjoying what you're doing. Guys, if you are controlling the toy, look your partner in the eye and ask: Faster? Slower? Pressure? Penetration? Don't just try to read her moans or silence as pleasure or boredom. And take your time! Dildos are often longer than the average erect penis, so be careful with vigorous thrusting, or you'll mash her cervix! Which hurts!!

"Lickety Split"

Dildos and cunnilingus. What a combo! Together with a dollop of water-based lube (flavored lube masks the purity of the girl juice), you'll both be in seventh heaven.

Guys: As your tongue begins to work its magic, begin teasing the insides of her thighs with the toy. Remember that anticipation is your most powerful seduction sauce. Now lube up the tip, and bring it to the vaginal opening. Don't stop licking! Slowly penetrate, moving the toy deeper or until she tells you you've found the right spot. Some women like simply being filled up, others like gentle or vigorous thrusting. Remember, communication is the key, so ask! Now gyrate the dildo while you keep licking, you unbelievable sex god!

"Combo Plate"

Lying on your back with your lover beside you, have him reach over with the lubed dildo to rub your clitoris, vulva and vaginal opening. Then the thrusting begins. With his other arm supporting your neck, his hand can caress your breasts and gently pinch your nipples (if you like that.). Now he's free to stretch upward to kiss your mouth, neck and delicately lick the edges or inside of your ear. The combination of the three point play is guaranteed to make you tingle!

"Squatter's Rights"

On a clean, smooth, hard, horizontal surface—like bathroom tile—place a few plush towels under your knees, and stick a suction cup dildo to the floor. Using lots of lube, penetrate yourself, grinding up and down. From behind, encourage your lover to caress your favorite erogenous zones—the back of your neck, behind your ears, breasts, nipples, clitoris—even fondle and gently pull your hair, or clutch your hips and help you with the pumping action. A vibrator is an excellent addition to this scenario. Your lover will love watching you.

"Worship Me"

With your lover kneeling before you, raise one leg up on a sturdy chair or coffee table. Have your lover penetrate you with a well-lubed toy, while using the

other hand to stroke your clitoris. Thumb-stroking with gentle pressure is ideal, since his opposable thumb is at the perfect angle while offering longer manual endurance. Since his mouth should now be about breast-high, you're in perfect position for delicious nipple sucking and breast kissing. As he varies the speed and pressure creatively, the worship will pay off.

From G-spot to *Gee!*-spot— How To Find It

Many women reach adulthood without ever discovering the orgasmic potential of the G-spot—yet it's a highly erogenous area that can give you very special orgasms.

To locate your G-spot, insert a finger just inside your vaginal opening, hooking your fingertip slightly as if to make a "come here" gesture. Just past the edge of the pubic bone, feel for a small spongy area under the surface of the upper part of your vaginal wall.

If you don't find it immediately—don't worry—it's there. You'll probably have to try different types of stimulation to turn it on. In fact, many women who know where to find their G-spot still need the help of a toy or their partner to get maximum pleasure from it. So relax, take a deep breath, and start exploring.

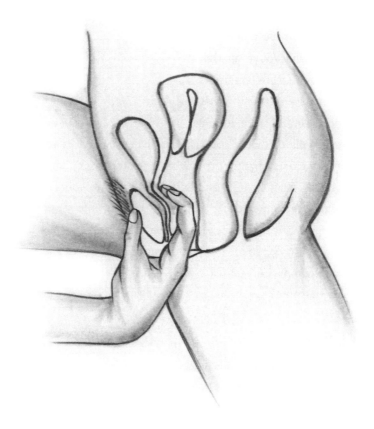

Once you've located your G-spot, you're in for a whole new type of orgasmic fun—and there are many special toys created especially for it, so you can unlock your G-spot orgasms in ways your fingers can hardly match.

"G-Wiz"

If your G-spot is your gee-spot—and you're also an oral sex lover—ecstasy is about to rise to a whole new level. Obtain a curved  glass dildo that's got a glass ball at each end. After lubricating the toy with a water-based lube, grab a sturdy hold of one end, and penetrate yourself with the other till it is firmly nestled into your G-spot. Then delicately rotate the arched toy to the side, giving your lover just enough access to lick and lap your pleasure button—all while you're still hitting the G-spot.

"Gia Pet"

If you've never experienced internal and external G-spot stimulation at the same time, get ready for a new orgasmic experience. Start with a firm, well-lubed G-spot dildo. As you both work it up inside you till it's pleasurably in place against your G-spot, have your lover place his hand above your mons veneris and apply firm inward pressure toward your pubic bone. This will compress the area slightly, increase

Dildos—Ready When You Are

pressure on your G-spot, and send you through the skylight (if you didn't have a skylight before, you will now!). Continue on with creative exploration, such as clitoral massage and oral love. ❤

5

Toygasms!

6 Vibrators— Get Your Buzz On!

Vibrator: *Any device or sex toy that has an electrical or mechanical movement designed to arouse or soothe. Vibrators come in a variety of shapes for topical use, or phallic-shaped for topical use and penetration.*

Vibrators can open a whole new world of pleasure in your sex life. They're perfect for delivering intense pleasure to the clitoris and vulva, with a level of stimulation and orgasm-inducing power unlike any other toy.

Vibrators come in a variety of designs, from body massagers to lifelike double-headed thangs to special gloves with vibrating fingertips. Available in two broad categories, plug-in electrical vibrators tend to be more powerful (and won't lose juice at critical moments!), while battery-powered models are smaller, more portable, less expensive and even waterproof.

You can use a vibrator to lightly massage your muscles and body parts, or to directly stimulate your erogenous zones. Many women achieve intense orgasms much more quickly with vibrators than with manual methods. Vibrators also help create a more powerful build-up to orgasm, allowing you to finish with another preferred technique. And while you might be perfectly satisfied with a different method for achieving orgasms, why not give vibrators a try? Variety is the spice of life!

Electric Vibrators: Plug In—Turn On

No batteries required—just plug these "personal massagers" into the wall and you're off! You'll find quality brand-name models at department stores, electronic gizmo shops and lingerie boutiques—although sales staff will be more knowledgeable at reputable sex toy shops (and you'll be less embarrassed asking!). These shops also stock the widest range of accessories.

Electric models provide extreme pleasure to your entire body, not just your erogenous zones. You'll enjoy their penetrating and diffuse vibrations, whether it's to soothe your aching back, or your aching loins. They tend to be larger than battery-operated models, and much more powerful, so be sure to take your time before working up to full vaginal or penile contact. And of course, keep them out of the bathtub or shower!

Hand Wands

The most popular and recognizable electric model, hand wands are less than a foot long, with an easy-to-grip handle and a vibrating head about the size of a tennis ball. You can control the frequency of the vibrations, either soft or fast in some models, or like a dimmer switch in other models. Start off easy! The fast speeds can be uncomfortable in the beginning, but the slow vibrations can be heavenly. Set your vibrator to slow, and tease the insides of your thighs before making direct contact with your clitoris. Also consider placing a wash cloth in between yourself and the vibrator or keeping your panties on when you first try it—the vibrations could be too intense.

Hand wands deliver such an intense vibration, they are often the right prescription for pre-orgasmic women to help them achieve their first orgasms. They can also help postmenopausal women bring their libido back to life.

Pleasure-amplifying attachments are made specifically for these models and fit over the ball-shaped head. For women, there are straight, smooth 3" to 4" phallic shapes, or a curved design that reaches your G-spot. Many women claim this simultaneous clitoral and G-spot stimulation to be the best. For men, options include a special "cup" attachment to stimulate the head of the penis which makes for thunderous orgasms.

Double Headers

If you like strong simultaneous genital and anal stimulation, these models will give you the jolts of a lifetime. Double headed electric models resemble the standard hand wands, but with two tennis ball-sized heads and plenty of vibrating power. And the heads are spaced just right for the vigorous dual-action workout you crave.

Swedish Pleasurizers

For skin-to-skin contact, strap this classic design over the back of your hand and let your fingers and palm vibrate you to orgasmic bliss. Men have used this model with success, although it makes the stroking action a bit cumbersome. For women who love to masturbate with their fingers, but want a new variation that's easier to use than a Swedish massager, check out the Finger Fitters in this chapter.

Whispering Coils

Shhhh. If noise is an issue, plug in a coil-electric vibrator. Its tantalizing vibrations come from an electromagnetic coil, and some models even resemble a small hair dryer. Experiment with the half-dozen or so attachments for playful variety and precise stimulation. Now you can be assured that your vibrator will be whisper quiet—but will YOU?

 Sadie Sez:

An electric vibrator is a golden treasure for women who have trouble orgasming.

Battery-Powered Vibrators:
Have Juice—Will Travel

Imagine...vibrators without the tether of an electric cord! Today's popular battery-powered sex toys come in an amazing array of shapes, sizes and colors, ready to deliver the extraordinary pleasure you want. Several attachments even let you customize your toy by changing its shape and texture, and special sleeves allow you to insert it for wild new tingly sensations. Experiment and surprise yourself!

Portables don't always have the vibration power of plug-ins, but you won't be disappointed at the power and features available today. You'll find most battery-powered models offer several speeds—or you can opt for the variable control switch, and set your own vibration frequency exactly how you like it. The latest models offer even more bells and whistles—like pulsation patterns and intensity control—which sounds like overkill at first, until you give them a try! Some models come with a hand-held controller connected to the toy by a wire—giving your partner a fun device to ramp up your pleasure. But self-contained units make one-handed solo play a lot easier, leaving your other hand free to roam.

Keep in mind that the type of vibration or movement tends to create greater pleasure than the size of the toy. The challenge is finding the models that satisfy you. Start by considering what you really want: portability, bathtub play, realism, simultaneous vaginal/clitoral or vaginal/anal stimulation—then let your imagination run wild! I'll help you sort it out.

Love Eggs

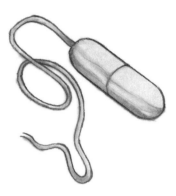

For powerful clitoral sensations, egg-shaped vibrators are the first choice among most women. Sometimes called bullet vibrators, they come in many oval shapes, from slimmer to longer and rounder. Plenty of colors, too. You control your own sensations with a small hand-held device as you cradle and move the egg all over your clitoris. They're not designed for insertion, but lots of other models are.

 Sadie Sez:

With an egg pressed against your chin or cheeks, your whole face and tongue become an instant vibrator. Got any ideas what you might do now??

Ol' Reliables

Cylindrical vibrators are among the most commonly used vibrators. Some are smooth, others look like an erect penis, but either way, they provide a steady stream of external and internal stimulation. They usually range in size from four to eight inches long, and approximately one and a quarter inches in diameter. You'll usually find the variable speed control at the base.

Realistic

Similar to the lifelike dildos in the previous chapter, these vibrators have many of the anatomical features of an actual penis: veins, realistic skin texture, testicles—The Works! They add a nice twist for those who love their penetration with vibration and the touch of realism.

Contours

Designed to create softer, gentler clitoral sensations, contours are smooth, made of plastic or jelly, and appear very feminine. They're perfect if you have a very sensitive clitoris.

Mini-Massagers

About the size of a lipstick case, these tiny units get their power from a single AA battery—but don't let the size and basic features fool you. These discreet little vibrators are popular because they pack some mighty orgasms for women on the run. You can also get a selection of clitoral attachments for added fun. And for shower play, mini-massagers come in waterproof models.

Dual-Action

For maximum stimulation, many women swear by their dual-action vibrator. Why? Just imagine pleasuring yourself with a shaft that vibrates AND rotates—as well as presses a small vibrating rubber animal on your clitoris. These could be the most intense orgasms you've ever had—thanks to a tiny rabbit, panther or dolphin! Other models have pearl-like plastic balls that circulate inside the shaft to stimulate your nerve endings at the entrance. Newer models have metal balls on a corkscrew

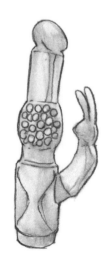

track that provide a feeling of ongoing penetration—
while you control the motion, speed and frequency. Just
choose your favorite color, material, shape, model,
size—and animal!

Note: When selecting a dual-action vibe, check
the length of the shaft—some can be too long,
preventing you from properly using the clitoral
stimulator at the base.

Advanced Pulsars

If you're wondering what the future
holds for sex toy play, look no further
than these advanced models, complete
with an LED screen to display your
settings. Now you can set your
pleasure exactly the way you like it:
one control to adjust the intensity; the
other to regulate the vibrations, from
throbbing to pulsating, rotating and
gyrating. Even though these are among
the pricier models, they provide more
variety in settings and uses, so you
don't need several different toys for
different pleasures when you can have
them all in one. Think of all the money

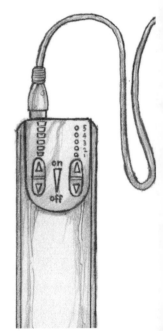

you'll save by staying home every night with your new pal!

Clitoral Pleasurizers

Although almost any vibrator will feel pretty good directly on your clitoris, there are plenty of models designed specifically for this little pleasure treasure. You can choose among basic one-point pleasure stimulators (like mini-massagers), or

vibrators with exotic split-action tips that stimulate the sides of your clitoris (like rabbit ears or animal paws)!

G-spot Seekers

If you're a G-spot lover, then you can probably spot a G-spot toy a mile away. They come semi-realistic or smooth, with that special bend in the shaft that connects with your magic spot. If you feel you've never really found your G-spot, or can't get enough stimulation there with your fingers, these toys are for you. And guys: they're ideal for an explosive effect on your prostate when inserted anally.

Finger Fitters

Do you like vibrators but miss the fingerplay? Now you can have both with these tiny vibrators that fit over your fingertips. Wear

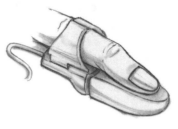

just one, or as many as ten! And if you like shower or hot tub play, there are even submersible gloves for hot underwater action.

Sneak-A-Thrill Undies

Sitting at your desk, on the train, in the park—or in the midst of 60,000 screaming sports fans—now you can have mind-blowing orgasms right then and there. (And if you can somehow manage to stay quiet, only you will know.) These specially designed panties have a small pocket sewn in front to hold your favorite love egg vibrator. And they're available in lots of exotic colors and animal prints to match your mood, as well as in a

Brazilian cut or thong to match your outfit. Secretly adjust the vibration power, and buzz your way to waves of intimate pleasure wherever you want!

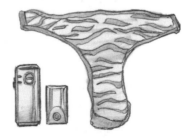

Hands-Free

If you just like to lie back and enjoy the ride, this hand's-free model is for you. Strap the elastic belt around your pelvis, position the stimulator on your clitoris, and vary the vibrations to your own desires with the hand-held  controller. Many models are just for clitoral stimulation— and can look like butterflies or bumblebees—while others come with vibrating penetrators for clitoral as well as vaginal and G-spot stimulation.

 Sadie Sez:

Try a hands-free clitoral stimulator with your man during intercourse for the time of your life!

Remote-Control Thrills

Guys: imagine being able to get your woman off at the touch of a button. If you're both intrigued by the

element of surprise, have your woman wear a remote-control vibrator. Then, like a TV clicker, you can control the action— only now you control the vibrations that set-off her explosive orgasms. Models

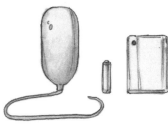

are available in panty, bullet and hands-free styles. What a wild stocking-stuffer!

Clitoral Pumps

A recent innovation for women who want to unblock their orgasm potential— as well as all those who crave powerful orgasms—is a small pump that creates a suction around the clitoris, along with some tantalizing vibrations. Just be sure to follow the directions and carefully regulate the suction from getting too strong, or it could damage your sensitive organ.

Let's Accessorize!

Here's how to refine your vibrator into the custom toy that's perfect for you:

Vibrators—Get Your Buzz On!

💜 *Sleeves.* Place an outer sleeve over your favorite hard plastic or smooth vibrators and start enjoying multiple sensations from a single toy. You'll find them in smooth, semi-realistic and realistic finishes—either as part of a cost-effective kit or sold separately.

💜 *Waterproofing.* If you're into waterplay, you can find most battery-powered vibrators in waterproof styles, too. Now you don't have to leave your favorite toys behind when you get into the bathtub or hot tub.

💜 *In-and-out action.* These "strokers" simulate the in-and-out action of penetration—all on their own!

💜 *Shapes.* Vibrators come in hundreds of fun shapes and sizes—even cute animals and your astrological sign!

💜 *Mood toys.* Some toys actually change color when they come in contact with your body heat. Other toys activate by touch or contact with moisture.

💜 *Self lube.* A few toys self-lubricate while vibrating, saving you from interrupting your pleasure to keep everything slippery-smooth.

💜 *Stealth.* Nearly silent toys help keep your activities private, except for the occasional moan or groan.

💜 *Rechargeable.* Some vibrators come with their own recharger base, so they're always ready when you are.

How To Choose Your Perfect Vibrator Discreetly

Consult this checklist to help you get the most pleasure from your new "friend":

♥ *Function.* Start by asking yourself how you plan to use the toy: overall vulva, clitoris, G-spot, anally, or more?

♥ *Use.* Are you planning to enjoy it on your own, or with someone very special?

♥ *Location.* On your way to work, on business trips, or simply after a long day, in your own tub or bed?

♥ *Noise.* Thin walls? Nosy neighbors? Curious room-mates? Controlling parents? Go for quiet.

♥ *Portability.* Do you want a toy that slips discreetly into your purse or backpack, or a plug-in model that mostly stays home?

♥ *Design.* Do you like the look and texture of a real penis, or prefer a completely different appearance?

♥ *Frequency.* Do you like slow or fast, deep or shallow? Get your hands on different units to see how they feel.

♥ *Price.* Aren't you worth a few extra dollars for all the free orgasms you're going to enjoy? Don't skimp on pleasure—get what will satisfy you!

Zesty Vibrator Tricks: On Your Own

"The Big Tease-y"

If you're new to vibrators, start here. What makes this technique so powerful is you're going to tease yourself for as long as you can stand it. Set the toy to a gentle vibration. Now slooowwwly caress the vibrator against the insides of your thighs, up across your belly, then circle your nipples—just teasing (but not touching) your vulva as you pass it by. Gradually move the toy down there as you become aroused, while making larger "figure 8" motions across your body.

When you ache for more, concentrate the movements into to smaller and smaller "figure 8" patterns across your body until you reach your vulva. Now put some lube on the tip of the vibrator and draw slow, lazy "figure 8" motions around your clitoris, then down around the labia minora, and back up to your clitoris. Gradually increase the vibration to the frequency that feels oh so right.

"Magic Fingers"

We're going to turn your fingers into magical pleasure points. Ready?

Hold a bullet vibrator in the valley between your thumb and finger. Now turn on your vibe and stroke your pleasure points with your vibrating fingertips, letting the familiar feeling of your fingers take on a new dimension. Adjust the vibrations to match your cravings and rub with your favorite clitoral techniques. Enjoy the

"Side Winder" technique and glide your buzzing fingers vertically, up and down, stimulating your sensitive inner labia as well as your clitoris.

"Double Your Pleasure"

Have you ever thought of using two toys at the same time? Inserting a dildo while stimulating your

clitoris with a vibrator feels heavenly—and very different than just a dildo and a finger. Try experimenting with different combinations and stroking techniques, or simply leave the dildo inside you while you work your magic with the vibrator. Don't forget plenty of lube!

Now try different toy movements, such as a "Figure 8" around your clitoris—or "Twist 'n Shout" from the dildo chapter. Or reverse the technique: penetrate yourself with the vibrator and rub the head or shaft of the dildo on your clitoris. You might not emerge from your bedroom for a week!

"Upside-Down Rabbit Trick"

Dual-action vibrators are total satisfiers in their normal position: shaft inserted, pearls rotating at the vaginal entrance, rabbit-eared stimulator buzzing away on your sweet spot. There's a reason sales of these toys continue to hum!

But have you ever thought to rotate the shaft 180 degrees, so the rabbit ears quiver and vibrate against your sensitive areas, now including your perineum— that sensitive stretch of skin between your vagina and anus? Well, why not?

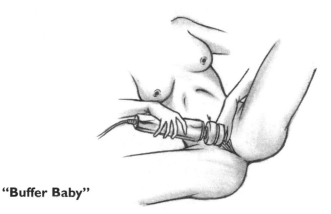

"Buffer Baby"

Many women crave full-force vibrations on the clitoris for toe-curling orgasms, but for others this is too intense. If you prefer a more subtle vibration, try this:

Position three of your fingers side by side right over your clitoris. Place the vibrator on the back of your fingers, and press. Adjust the vibration to your liking, and press some more. This will give you mind-blowing stimulation of the clitoris, but with a softer vibration. *Mmmmm.*

Sadie Sez:

When you rotate your toy, any speed and vibration controls in the base will be upside-down, too. So pre-set them before you flip it over!

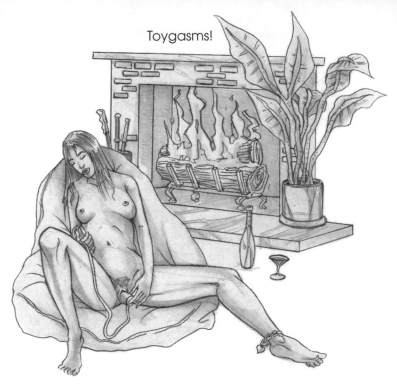

"Slip 'n Slide"

Want your toy do more of the work? Start by lubing up and turning on a penetrating-type vibrator. Now tease your clitoris with just the tip—and enjoy your first orgasm before going deeper.

Now slowly work the toy in by gently twisting it so the vibrations lead the way. Play with the setting till you find your perfect 'moan' intensity, and hold it inside you with your fingers at the bottom. Now release your fingers and feel the vibrator naturally start to slide out. Let it go a few inches, then firmly thrust it back in again. Explore different angles, and hit your G-spot by aiming upward. Repeat over and over again with short, firm thrusts, and even use your free hand for tantalizing clitoral stimulation as you go slip slidin' away!

Vibrator Thrills For Lovers

"Sit-n-Buzzzzzzz"

Get comfortable. Get naked. Get out your egg vibrator, along with some lube and a sturdy chair (no wheels!).

Sit on your lover's lap with your legs outside his. Have him reach around in front of you with the pre-lubed toy and nuzzle it in between your labia, nicely against your clitoris—just the way you like it. He's now free to explore your breasts and inner thighs with his free hand—and you're free to grind delightfully into him. And, when you feel his sexy enticing bulge beneath you, consider a grand entrance from behind, while he kisses, sucks and nibbles the back of your neck.

"Eye 2 Eye"

If you haven't gazed into your lover's eyes during sex, you're missing out on a deep intimate connection and an abundance of personal pleasure.

Try this: dim the lights to a comfortable level. Facing your lover on the bed, lie back with your legs straddling his thighs, giving him a full erotic view of your beautiful,

naked body. In this position, he can arouse you with a well-lubed vibrator while your eyes stay locked on each other's. Use your own hands to caress your breasts, or play with a nipple toy. Relax and enjoy the wonderful clitoral sensations your lover is giving you. And if you're lucky, he may use his fingers to play you know where!

"Finger Vibing"

Guys: All you need is an electric wand vibrator and your two talented hands. With your lover lying on her back, facing you, sit comfortably between her legs. Now turn your palm up, place the head of the vibrator into that

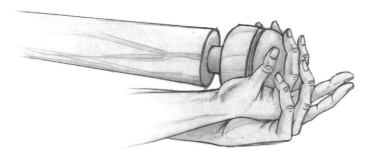

hand, and grip it. Place your other palm directly underneath your hand and cradle it, along with the buzzing vibrator. Now extend both middle fingers, and maneuver your hands around until you've got the perfect finger-on-finger positioning. After she lubes up your fingers, start stimulating! You've just invented a fleshy finger vibrator full of all the tricks and twists you can imagine. Now curve your fingers up and create a natural G-spot vibrator. Go forth and explore!

"Mt. Ecstasy"

If you like your sex "doggie style," why not add a touch of vibration that begs for more.

Assume the position, either on your hands and knees, or your elbows and knees, or with your chest to the bed and butt in the air. As your lover mounts you from behind, have him reach around with a well-lubed toy to stimulate your clitoris while you're sensually moving with him. This may take a little balance control, but once you're in rhythm, you'll also be in heaven. There's nothing quite like a little vibration on your clitoris while you're enjoying that glorious feeling of fullness from behind.

"Bionic Manhood"

Ladies: Kneeling in front of your naked guy, lube up his penis and caress him with his favorite stroking styles—swift and strong or gentle and slow. Now take a small cylindrical vibrator, set it to low, and place it either at the bottom of his shaft, or right beneath his testicles. Don't stop stroking. Be sure to soak in every expression and reaction from the new and oh-so-pleasurable feelings you're giving him.

Guys: Here's where you become the Bionic Man. With both of you standing, take control of the vibrator. Hold it in place at the bottom of your shaft, and begin rubbing the head of your penis *sloooowly* against her

Toygasms!

clitoris and labia. The vibrations—together with the slippery smooth texture of your head—will send shivers of pleasure through both of you. ♥

Tanya, a 47-year-old married woman with two kids, always thought the faint orgasms with her husband Jack were adequate. "One of my girlfriends gave me a vibrator as a birthday gift," she says. "I'd never tried a vibrator before, but I was so curious. I decided to give it a try, especially since Jack had taken the kids to the zoo. And wow! What powerful orgasms! I never imagined they could feel so good. I was stunned by all the years gone by where I thought I'd been satisfied. When I got up the nerve, I delicately introduced it into the bedroom, and now Jack's got a few new tricks up his sleeve! My orgasms will never be the same. Thank the Lord!!"

 Sadie Sez:

Be sure to insert your batteries correctly by matching the + and - signs inside the battery compartment.

To extend your battery (and toy) life, take out the batteries and store them separately between uses.

7 The Anal Playground

Anal toy: *Any object designed to pleasure the anus, whether on the surface or by penetration.*

Do you find anal play pleasurable? Have you ever tried it with a partner—or solo? Don't be intimidated. Contrary to myth, if you follow a few safety guidelines, back door play can be quite a treat. In fact, whether you enjoy delicate fingertip pressure at the opening, or penetration with fingers, dildos or a plug, it can be extremely stimulating.

You may not orgasm from anal stimulation alone, but together with clitoral or vaginal play, you'll enjoy stronger, more exhilarating orgasms. There's a wide world of tempting, creative toys available today to enhance your experience—and undoubtedly there's a perfect model for you!

Feeling Adventurous? Read This First:

Communicate

Anal play is a perfectly healthy desire in men and women. Talking about anal play—before, during and after—always helps enhance your experience and avoid physical discomfort. Be sensitive to your partner's feelings; don't pressure beyond anyone's comfort zone, and respect all likes and dislikes.

Remember: communication, patience and proper technique add up to highly stimulating fun!

Lube up

Unlike the vagina, there's no natural lubrication produced in the anus and rectum. This means you must add your own lubrication before engaging in this activity—even more than you think necessary. Silicone lubes are ideal for back door play, since they stay slippery longer than water-based lubes and generally have a thicker texture.

Cleanliness

Never insert a finger or sex toy you've used for anal play into your vagina until you've washed the digit or toy thoroughly with anti-bacterial soap and hot water. Transferring bacteria from one area to another could cause infection. No back-and-forthing without washing!

Safety

Your rectum is lined with thin, delicate tissue. It's why you need to inspect anything you plan to put in there for rough edges that may scratch or tear the lining. Your fingernails must be well-trimmed and filed smooth. And feel your toys for even the slightest seams—then smooth any rough edges with a nail file.

Relax. And then relax even more

Relax your mind. Relax your body. And most of all, relax your sphincters! This allows the tissue folds of the anal canal to expand, making them more receptive to penetration. It's also your key to enjoying the experience. Let yourself go in all ways, and revel in the sensations of the erotic touch to your most densely concentrated nerve endings. You'll shiver in delight.

Go sloooow

You're playing with tissue that's very thin—much more delicate than the walls of a vagina. Go slow. Be gentle. And create the perfect technique to enhance the unique sensations of anal play.

How To Find The Best Anal Toys For You

That depends on what you like. Some women like the pleasures of simultaneous anal and vaginal penetration. Others like the sense of "fullness" from plug insertion during intercourse, which also tightens the vagina and stimulates more pleasure for both partners. And many men like the way an anal plug stimulates the prostate during lovemaking, which can lead to more explosive orgasms. You'll find what works best for you in this chapter.

Sadie Sez:

Wrap your toy in two or three condoms and simply remove an outer condom when switching from anus to vagina, or from one partner to another.

Choose Your Anal Toy Style

Butt Plugs

Put 'em in—and leave 'em in. These anal toys come in a variety of different sizes, but all have a similar shape— narrow at the base, thickest in the middle and narrowest on top. The flared base prevents the plug from

getting "sucked in" and lost inside the rectum. Plugs are designed to stay still while inside, rather than be pushed in and out. It will help you train and relax your anal muscles, and give you a pleasurable feeling of fullness as you stimulate your other erogenous zones.

"Corkscrew You"

Go "corkscrew" yourself! These butt plugs are designed to do just what they say, featuring ridges that curve around the toy from top to bottom—just like a screw. After lubing the toy, lightly twist it inside you with an upward pressure. Feel the ridges caress the sphincter muscles as the toy slowly moves inside. Take your time, tease the sensations, and continue corkscrewing yourself till the plug is at its last ridge, all tight and snug inside. When you're done, reverse the motion to remove the plug.

Vibrating Butt Plugs

For a little buzz in your tush, try a vibrating butt plug during solo or partner sex. These plugs come with a variable-speed vibrator that you activate from a hand-held controller. The feeling of fullness, together with a touch of inner vibration, create unusual, exciting sensations.

Anal Beads

These smooth orgasm-enhancing beads come in all sizes—from blueberry-small to orange-gigantic! They're made of plastic, jelly, rubber or silicone, and are strung together with nylon or cotton cords. Just pre-insert a strand of lubed beads into the anus, then slowly pull them out during orgasm. Many men and women enjoy the feeling of the anus opening and closing around each bead during orgasmic

contractions. *Note:* Cotton cord models are for one-time use only, since they can store bacteria, even after washing. Go nylon or silicone instead.

"Moon Beads"

Inserting anal beads can be just as much fun as pulling them out. Pre-lube them, then slowly, gently, nudge each one in, keeping the pull-ring outside. You may really enjoy watching them feed into your lover's back door, knowing you'll soon be popping them back out! When

 Sadie Sez:

Before using anal beads, always examine them thoroughly for any rough edges that may need filing and smoothing.

the climactic moment arrives, ease them out by gently tugging on the ring. Your lover will feel the exciting orgasmic contractions hug each bead with the outward motion. Swifter extractions can be pleasing for some, but play it safe and work up to that gradually.

Anal Probes

For a more active anal experience, try these slender vibrating or non-vibrating probes. Some  are made with flexible materials, others are available as a stiff, gyrating model. And some models offer a series of gentle mounds on the shaft that allow the anus to expand and contract as the probe is moved in and out.

Inflatable Toys

Now you can start small and increase your pressure and pleasure progressively—especially during intercourse! Just use the small hand pump to inflate this toy after it's in position. These toys also serve to 'fill up' space in your rectum, so your vagina may feel 'tighter' to your man.

Anal Toy Pleasure Tricks

"XXX-tasy"

More and more women are enjoying a little back-door play together with their vibrator play. All you need is a vibrator, a small butt plug, and plenty of lube.

Get comfortable on the couch, lying on your back or side with one leg up. Lubricate the vibrator, and begin buzzing with your favorite clitoral stroking styles. Once your juices are flowing, lube up your butt plug,

and begin caressing your relaxed anus with its tip. Feel the ticklish, yet erotic sensations from the responsive nerve endings. When you're ready, gently probe inward with the plug—you may find it's already working its own way in! You'll love the feeling of fullness from behind, together with the heavenly clitoral stimulation from your vibrator.

"Take Me Away"

Go for something new and naughty. And naughty in a good sense—since it's just you and your lover. Lay on

your side, with him behind you in a spoon-like position. As you rub your favorite lube all over your inner vulva and clitoris, allow him to pleasure you from behind, using his fingers in creative ways and places. There's nothing like your guy's loving fingers inside you while you're taking care of the outer pleasure spot at the same time. After you've had an orgasm or two, have him lube up his finger and play around your anus. Remember, this is to be done slowly, sensually and with lots of lube. When the exotic probing of a single finger is getting you off, he can go for two fingers, or graduate to a small anal dildo! ♥

Sadie Sez:

Most people stash their pleasure treasures in the nightstand, but what if they could be "found" there by curious kids and nosy guests? Try this: hide your toys in a shoebox under the mattress, or zippered inside a special pillow with secret inner pockets. Opaque plasticware from your kitchen offers you another safe option. Best yet, hang a draw-string bag on a hanger in your closet, between two of your own garments. No one will EVER find them there!

8 Playthings For Nipples

Are you among the lucky women whose breasts, nipples and areolas are nearly as sensitive as your labia, clitoris and vagina—or just as responsive? If you haven't experimented with all the playthings designed for nipples, especially during lovemaking, this chapter will change your outlook!

Nipple play for many women and men is a tantalizing treat. And you'll find an assortment of toys that deliver mild-to-wild sensations that can mimic the tease of a lover's nibble—to the squeeze of a lover's bite. The key to your enjoyment? Go slow. Whether your toy has a wide, flat surface to give you a broad, dull sense of pressure, or a thumbscrew to give you eye-watering tension, experiment with different parts of your nipples till you find your own erotic spots.

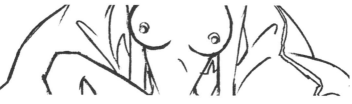

Nipple Clamps

Nipple clamps are heavenly for the nipple-play connoisseur. They come with many different pleasure-enhancing features, such as rubber or vinyl tip-covers to keep you comfortable while protecting you from too much pressure. You'll also find adjustable clamps, vibrating clamps, and clamps that heat up. Other models feature attractive chains that connect one clamp to the other, so you can gently tug on them for extra sensations.

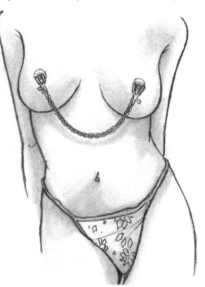

"Dragon Bite"

Start by discovering which parts of your nipples give you the most erotic sensations. Some people like the clamps on the very tips of their nipples, while others prefer them at the base. Tighten the grip so you feel the sharp, yet enjoyable sensation—which may repeat each time you move or jiggle the toy. Now, with your clamps in place, begin your solo or partner sex-play. When you're ready to release the clamps, you may feel that sharp sensation again, but this time it's caused by the blood flowing back into your nipples—a big erotic rush! Repeat clamping and releasing to your pleasure during each nipple-play session.

Suction Toys

You can choose from two types of nipple suction toys: static and hand-activated pumps. Static toys are suction cups or vinyl caps that fit over your nipples. After moistening the edge with lube or saliva, squeeze the sides and place one over each nipple for a suction-y grip.

Hand-activated nipple pumps will give you more suction sensations, but often work on just one nipple at a time, and it can get in the way during lovemaking. *Warning:* Do not use a nipple pump on your clitoris. It could damage your delicate organ. ♥

 Sadie Sez:

If you're a new mother with a breast-feeding milk pump, I don't need to remind you they also make great nipple suction toys!

Toygasms!

9 Rousing Toys For Daring Boys

I s your fearless macho man actually intimidated by a widdle wubba penis ring? Did you know lots of guys today relish these and other boy-toys? Millions of dollars flow each year into the adult trade for toys and accessories for guys—which gives new meaning to the term "stocking stuffer!" So show this section to your guy, and see which toys light up his tree.

Rings

Also known as "cock rings," these gadgets wrap tightly around the base of a man's tool—or around both testicles and the base of his penis—to help him maintain a

harder, longer-lasting erection. Rings also put pressure on the contracting muscle during climax, giving what some guys describe as the strongest orgasms of their lives.

Most rubber and polyurethane rings are really stretchy, so they can easily be pulled wide open to accommodate even the biggest man, and later removed easily. Others have a slipknot design to enable easy positioning and tension adjustment, even during intercourse. Denim, leather and metal rings are popular, as well as newer materials such as super-stretchy silicone and other lifelike materials.

Many models feature erotic ticklers, so each thrust from a lover's penis delivers extra stimulation to the woman's clitoris and labia. Double tickler models stimulate the testicles, too. And some rings even come with multiple interconnected restraint rings to stretch or tug the testicles.

Note: Penis rings have a pleasure limit. To play it safe, don't wear them longer than 30 minutes at a time. Too much blood pressure inside the penis for too long can damage its delicate tissue and vessels. And if you're new at this, be sure to start with rings that remove easily.

"Ring Around The Collar"

Guys: If you enjoy making love with a ring around the base of your penis, try this sexy adventure with your lover. Place a ring comfortably in the middle of your shaft, then begin making love. See how she enjoys feeling you—plus the ring—stroking her inside with every thrust. You can even place the ring just beneath the head of your penis, so you can stimulate her G-spot. Or for a truly unique experience, wear multiple rings for an energizing speed-bump effect.

 Sadie Sez:

Many men masturbate wearing a penis ring for explosive orgasms!

Vibrating Penis Rings

Turn a real-life penis into a real live vibrator! A vibrating ring gives him explosive orgasms, while the

small egg-vibrator attachment offers her splendid hands-free clitoral stimulation. For variety, turn the ring upside-down so the egg stimulates his testicles. Or get the best of both worlds: a double-sided vibrating ring holds two eggs: one for each of you!

"Double Her Pleasure"

Guys: Reluctant to wear a vibrating penis ring? Then just attach a vibrating ring near the base of a dildo and let the toy deliver the joy! Penetrate your lady with the lubed, egg-bearing dildo, gently stroking her in and out, working it deep inside. The egg will vibrate against her clitoris for a climax she'll never forget. And what an incredible view for you!

Penis Pumps

Where nature may have short-changed a guy, penis pumps can make up for the shortfall—at least temporarily. Pumps work by creating a vacuum around the penis, which increases blood flow into the shaft. This enhances size and stiffness.

To extend the life of your pumped-up creation, place a ring around the base of the penis at the peak of hardness. Beware of cheaply made penis pumps. Look for higher-end pumps made with quality rubber or latex seals at the opening and powerful pistol-grips.

Sadie Sez:

Guys: For the best penis pump results, groom and trim your pubic area.

Ball Spreaders

For guys who don't mind messing around in "Man Land," ball spreaders are designed to strap around the base of the penis and scrotum, to lift and separate the testicles or stretch the scrotum. It provides a unique pleasure from gentle pulling, stretching and teasing— and can result in intense orgasms during solo or partner sex. They're made of leather or metal, with straps, rings and chains designed to spread the testicles. Most models snap on and off. For the truly adventurous, they also come with small weights to create a heavier, pulling sensation.

"It's A Snap!"

Adventurous guys: Attach a ball spreader with sequential snaps around the base of your penis and scrotum and begin solo or partner sex. You'll feel yourself getting bigger and harder as you approach climax. Then, on your mark, get set, go! With your first orgasmic contraction, grab and release a snap around one of your testicles, and feel the blood rush back into it with a deep, intense sensation. Repeat with the snap around the other testicle at another contraction. By the time you get to the snap around your penis, you may be on your way to what is often described as a male multiple orgasm.

Penis Thickeners

It's not always length, but girth that can be the real woman-pleaser. Many women enjoy the feeling of fullness that comes from sex with a meaty organ, and the adult toy industry has something for you.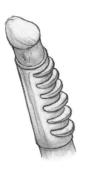
The latest penis thickeners are made of new lifelike materials that feel soft and real. Most of them leave the head of the penis exposed, with a tapered tip that flares out toward the base. So the deeper you go, the wider you go—till the woman is filled up and satisfied.

Pleasures Of The Prostate

The good news: all men have a highly erogenous zone that most aren't even aware of. *The better news:* many men have incredible orgasms purely by stimulating this sensitive area. *The not-so-good news:* the only way to reach it is through the rectum.

This pleasure center is the prostate. It's also known as the "male G-spot" because of similarities to its female counterpart. Walnut-sized, the prostate is located behind the pubic bone, under the bladder. It's the gland that produces ejaculatory fluid.

To stimulate the prostate manually, all you need is plenty of lube and a willing finger or toy to massage it. It's situated about three inches inside the rectum—you'll KNOW when you've struck gold. Simply give it firm pressure, massaging it toward the front of the body. This stimulates the root of the penis, where the nerve endings are located. Once a guy can learn to relax and get past any hang-ups about anal penetration, he'll be ready for explosive orgasms he never thought possible.

Vibrating Anal-Ts

Guys: If you'd like to experience what an internal erotic massage feels like, vibrating Anal-Ts are your answer.

They're designed to seek out your prostate—and satisfy like no other toy—because it's curved just right to land an exciting vibration right where you want it. For your comfort, Anal-Ts come in several different sizes, and with multi-speed vibrations.

Sadie Sez:

Ladies: Place an Anal-T inside your own back door during regular partner sex. Your lover will be able to feel the little vibrating "bump" on his penis with each stroke!

"The Oralizer"

Just like G-spot stimulation, prostate stimulation is usually better after your man is already aroused. Start by stroking his penis with one hand, while a lubed fingertip on your other hand teases his anus. Once he's all worked up, lube up a vibrating Anal-T and slowly work it inside him. Gently angle the toy so the tip is pointing toward his pubic bone, as it brushes against his prostate. The prostate is very sensitive, so you should be able to tell when you've found it. Now slowly massage his prostate while you use your other hand to get him off, and then give him the best oral sex of his life!

Nearly Real Vaginas

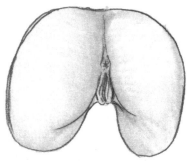

Imagine…a legal substitute for a vagina that's tight, safe, satisfying—and you don't even have to buy it dinner! Today's miracle compounds create a soft, lifelike feel that may even be molded from your favorite porn star's privates. Models include "vagina-only" or a double-your-pleasure "vagina-anus" combo. Other features include hand pumps, vibrating eggs and even a G-spot hidden inside. Quality varies, so shop around.

Cool Jerks

Small, compact "masturbation sleeves" are a guy's true pocket pal for instant hand jobs. Some are as simple as a latex tube—others come with small pearls embedded inside for added stimulation. You'll even find porn star-molded mouths eager to please you. The heavier masturbators are more durable, and many men claim they feel

more real. They're available in a variety of materials and sizes, and many even vibrate. Some women swear by these products to keep their guys satisfied when they're out of town!

"Rolling Pin"

Guys: Apply lots of lube inside your cool jerk and slip your penis inside. Now put your hands on both sides of the sleeve and roll it between the palms of your hands, like you're rolling bread dough. Once you've got the perfect rolling speed and rhythm, add an up-and-down motion. Continue your custom-tailored stroking till your bread is fully buttered!

Instant Extenders

Extenders resemble a long condom-like sheathe with a semi-realistic dildo tip. They can add 1.5" to 3" to the length of a penis, and come in a variety of colors and materials. Though some couples enjoy them, they can insulate the penis from sensation. A few drops of lube might help, but this can also cause the extender to slip off at the worst possible moment. Extenders can also be used on a vibrator or dildo as well as with vibrating attachments. ♥

10 Strap One On

Strap-on harnesses are designed to hold a dildo upright and rigid against the pubic bone—much like an erect penis. This enables you to penetrate your lover while your hands are free to roam. Although strap-ons have traditionally been popular in the lesbian and gay communities, they are quickly making their way into middle-American bedrooms. In fact, many strap-on owners today are straight women. Surprised? It's because more and more of their husbands and boyfriends want to enjoy the pleasures of prostate orgasms.

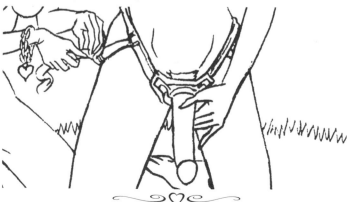

For women, wearing a harness can produce reactions like outright laughter or delicious feelings of sexual authority. For lesbian lovers, strap-ons can open up forms of pleasure unavailable by their natural anatomy. For straight men, these toys can be used to probe lovers anally and vaginally simultaneously. And for impotent men, as well as those who have trouble maintaining firm erections, a harness enables them to please their lovers infinitely.

Suit Your Every Need

The Dildo

Dildos expressly designed for harnesses come with a flared base so they'll always stay in position. Suction-cup dildos can work well, too. Just thread your dildo through the hole of the harness, strap the harness snugly against your body, and you're ready to play.

The Fit

Most good harnesses are made of garment-quality leather, latex or fabric, to provide the best positioning, flexibility and comfort. A good fit is essential, so be sure to shop for a harness that adjusts snuggly to your size. You simply connect the adjustable or elastic straps that wrap around your waist, legs and hips.

Strap One On

Single Or Double-Strap

Each version has its fans. Many women prefer single-strap styles, which resemble a G-string bikini. Men often prefer the double-strap styles, which connect the waistband to straps that go around the thighs. It's more practical for guys, because it runs to either side of the testicles and penis. This can also be more comfortable for women, too.

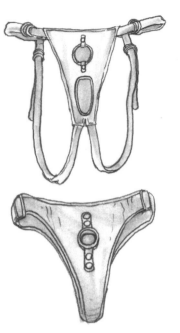

Sadie Sez:

If the straps or metal snaps on harnesses irritate your skin, wear a pair of men's boxer briefs or button-fly jeans under the harness.

The Opening

Many harnesses come together with matching dildos. And *a la carte* harnesses are often constructed to fit one dildo size only. If you already have a favorite dildo, be sure it will fit through the hole of the harness you're considering. Or seek out a harness that will accommodate various sizes of detachable support rings to hold your dildo firmly in place.

The Rings

Strap-on harness support rings come in metal, as well as in the more comfortable, flexible latex material. Some harness kits offer a limited one-size-fits-all ring, while others come with rings that snap on and off, increasing your dildo size options. If you plan on growing your dildo collection and exploring harness action, look for a harness with multiple ring options.

Head Gear

Headbands that position a dildo on your lover's chin may look bizarre, but think of the advantages: he can penetrate you vaginally while performing oral sex. It could even become an olympic event! Of course, it takes a little practice and a lot of neck muscles. But all joking aside, head gear also gives handicapped lovers new and exciting options for sexual pleasure.

Anywhere Gear

Popular with lesbian and bisexual women, these strap-ons allow you to place a dildo just about

anywhere! Use the lower part of your body such as your thigh or knee—or strap it to a chair! This allows for all kinds of creative lovemaking, especially when partners desire penetration while positioned face-to-face. ♥

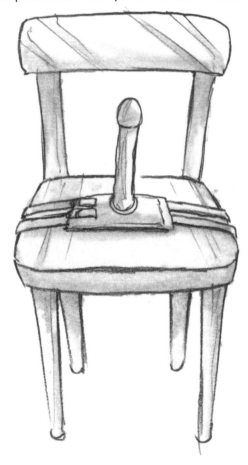

11

Curious Sex *Tchotchkes*

Before there were sex toys, there was nothing but everyday items found around the house and Old MacDonald's produce stand—plus lots of women with vivid imaginations. Today, these items still work their magic. The best thing about sex play with ordinary household objects is that once you know a few safety rules, you can really go creatively wild! The first rule to remember: always examine your play toys for any rough edges. Ready?

"The Wonders Of Indoor Plumbing"

If you've got a hand-held showerhead, adjust the water temperature and pressure to your liking, and direct the flow onto your clitoral area. It'll be easier if you place one foot up on the side of the tub, or onto a shower

seat, but be sure to keep your balance! The faster the flow, the more stimulating the effect, but start out with lower pressure and increase it as you become aroused. If your showerhead has a massage feature, adjust the pulsations to your liking, too. Many women can achieve orgasm quickly with direct waterjet stimulation. And if you've got a hot tub, you may very well know what powerful waterjet streams can do! Please be aware that highly pressurized streams of water into your vagina can cause irritation, so position yourself carefully.

"Niagara Falls"

Dim the lights. Draw the bath. Light the candles. Pour the wine. It's your time away from the pressures of daily life.

Set the water temperature and flow just the way you like it. Then lay beneath it and let it stream deliciously down on your clitoris. If you've got a suction cup dildo, attach it to the porcelain just under the faucet, and let it penetrate you as the water teases you. Your buoyancy in the water will help you glide it in and out. Use your hands and fingers to caress your breasts, clitoris and other body parts—or get a waterproof vibrating sponge. The vibes are so inconspicuous, so the kids will never know!

"Gum Massage"

Whiter teeth and fresher breath may be the slogan for lots of modern tooth-brushes, but how many will claim to give you a bright smile from an orgasm?

If you've got an electric toothbrush, you've also got an excellent vibrator all charged up and ready to go! Just cover the bristles with some plastic wrap or a con-dom, or bypass the brush and use the back of the vibrating tip on your clitoris. Electric toothbrushes only have one speed; hopefully it'll be the right frequency for you.

The Produce Section

It's quite a thrill to browse in the supermarket's produce section for a playtoy *du jour*. While everyone else is picking out salad ingredients for the family, you're sizing up cucumbers, carrots and bananas for an evening of organic pleasure. Be sure to select only the freshest ingredients, clean your selections carefully and trim off any rough sections. And don't overlook corn-on-the-cob in season—the rows of kernels are a healthy delight!

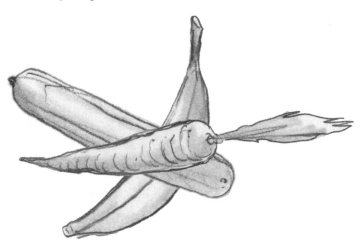

Random Acts of Pleasure

Are you suddenly inspired by phallic objects around the house? Then get creative! Candles, rubber handles and cooking utensils will all get the job done very well. Just be sure your new "toy" is clean and smooth and will wash up afterwards. And when a friend uses that spatula to flip your pancakes, you'll get added pleasure from knowing where it's been!

Washday Fun

Do you see laundry day as chore day? If it came with a whopping orgasm, would that change your outlook? Many women have discovered the simplicity of spin-cycle pleasure by sitting on a corner of their washing machine—or dryer—while the machines do the rocking and rolling for you. Recommended for home use only—hidden cameras in laundrymats could make you a star!

"Furniture Orgy"

Here's something you won't see in any furniture catalog: Armchair Sex!

Pick a soft chair or sofa with padded arms. Place a towel over one of the arms, then sit and carefully position yourself on the arm. Arch your back, spread

your legs, and let your vulva directly press against the arm. Roll your hips in small circles, or rub against the arm in quick back and forth motions. Wiggle around till you find that perfect position. When your clitoris is rockin', and you feel the blood flowin', that's Armchair Sex! ♥

Janine, a 28-year-old grad school student, discovered orgasmic fun with some ordinary household items, but didn't know if her toy choices were normal. "This may sound a little weird, but the handle on my hairbrush is perfect for reaching my G-spot, and the vibrations from my electric toothbrush really feel good on me, too."

"I was a little embarrassed to admit it, but a girlfriend of mine says that lots of women use household items, and it's perfectly normal. It's good to know I'm not some weirdo, and now I can enjoy myself without that uneasy feeling."

12 Let's Accessorize!

Accessories can often make the outfit, and it's no different for sex toys! Dressing up your toy can bring a you whole new level of excitement, better orgasms and pleasure—not to mention a few wicked laughs! In today's sex toy marketplace, there's an abundance of options for you to add extra oomph to your ol' pal.

Wand Add-On

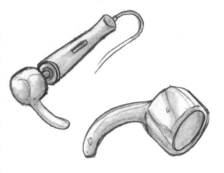

If you wish your wand vibrator came with a little more reach, try a "G-spotter." This attachment fits onto the head of your wand to reach your magic spot like nothing else. And the large vibrating ball will stimulate your clitoris at the same time!

Pleasure Swings

Wouldn't you love to suspend yourself in mid-air and feel the swoop of gravity as your lover penetrates you—or licks you—without fear of falling? Then you might want to try a pleasure swing. Hanging securely in a door frame, it allows you to fully control height, tilt and motion, so your lover can reach spots you didn't even know existed. If your bed, kitchen counter or massage table just aren't the right height, a pleasure swing is your perfect solution. Needless to say, carefully follow the swing's installation instructions.

Exercise Balls

You may have seen these big rubber balls at the gym for all kinds of exercises. Now you can bring them into your bedroom for all types of sexercises. Also known as Swiss Love Balls, they measure two-to-three feet in diameter, and give you and your lover a bouncy surface to explore new positions and let you penetrate deeper.

Serious Kegeling

If you want to tone your PC muscles for increased vaginal lubrication, stronger clitoral sensations, better vaginal grip and greater orgasmic abilities—here's the equipment to get you there.

You'll find different types of Kegel exercisers: some are made of surgical-grade steel which resemble a barbell and weigh a full pound! Others are made of plastic and resemble a forearm muscle toner. Whichever model you choose, insert it into your vagina and flex your PC muscles around it. This "weight lifting" increases blood flow to the area and tones your muscles to achieve your desired results.

Ben-Wa Balls

A product of Japanese tradition, you insert these marble-sized balls into your vagina for pleasure sensations, to exercise your PC muscles, or to enhance the effect of your vibrator! Imagine feeling these little balls inside you, jiggling around from a buzzing vibrator—or a pulsating motorcycle!

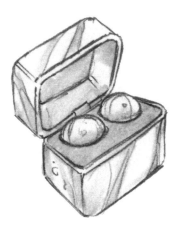

Ben-Wa balls are approximately three-quarters of an inch in diameter. They are made of non-porous materials, including acrylic, silver, steel, plastic and even gold-plated! *Note:* Ben-Wa balls are for vaginal play only—never insert them in your rectum where they could get lost. Also, beware if you're walking around with them inside you—they are notorious for slipping out at the wrong time!

Duotone Balls

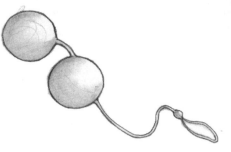

Larger, weighted, and some say more pleasurable than Ben-Wa balls, you insert duotone balls into your vagina to create a great range of pleasure sensations as you move. They come in sets of two or four golfball-sized spheres that are attached by a strong nylon string for easy removal and tugging. The motion is created when a weighted ball bearing inside each one rolls around freely as you walk, creating a subtle, but delicious sensation. And with a vibrator on your clitoris, the balls will quiver rapidly—shooting you to the moon!

"Disco Duck"

Duotone balls can be inserted before a night out on the town—with no fear of them falling out. So now you can boogie down on the dance floor and nobody has to know how you enhance those foot moves—unless you want them to!

Liquids, Lubes And Gels

Today you can find all kinds of massage oils and lotions—from slippery and unscented to warm and tasty. And you can

even select your slippery potion for your desired motion: erotic massage, anal play, self-pleasure or erection-enhancers!

♥ *Massage oils and lotions*. Massage oils and lotions come in a variety of scents and flavors: rose, lavender, almond, peach, or unscented. They are either mineral oil-based (so they stay slick for a long time), or glycerin-based (often flavored, but they can get sticky). Some actually heat up when you blow on them, but friction from a good rubbing will warm up most oils. Massage oils are not intended as a sexual lubricant—they can break down the latex in condoms and toys. And lotions tend to have sugar, which can cause yeast infections. For the best overall massage and lube combo, try a flavored lubricant.

♥ *Flavored lubes*. Perfect for tasty oral sex, you're sure to find a flavor you like: strawberry-kiwi, piña colada, watermelon chocolate and more. Some even have a cooling (mint) or warming (cinnamon) effect. As the name suggests, these lubes may taste good, but trace amounts of sugar can lead to yeast infections if introduced into the vagina.

♥ *Topical gels*. Feeling under-stimulated? Apply a topical gel to help increase the sensitivity of your clitoris, penis or nipples. Some gels have a cooling menthol effect. Others have active ingredients that dilate the blood vessels close to the surface. Once you apply a topical gel, it's absorbed into the skin and can be difficult to wash out. If this is your first time, start off with a small amount and see whether you like it.

♥ *Lickable liquids.* Hungry? Horny? Both? Try chocolate body paint, which melts at body temperature, or dash into the kitchen for some honey, syrup, molasses or whipped cream. Don't forget the maraschino cherries! Lickables are best used in the tub, where cleanup is easier, and your satin sheets and pillow cases are spared!

Sex Games

For the most satisfying dinner parties you've ever had, break out a sexy board game or role-playing game and let the fun begin. Widely available on the web and at adult boutiques, these games are designed for the bedroom, bathtub and even group play. Or break out a deck of cards and revive the game of strip poker.

Massage Mitts

For a tingly sensation that'll get your juices flowing, try a waterproof jelly massage mitt. Just lube up the outside, insert

Toygasms!

 Sadie Sez:

Place a vibrating egg in your massage mitt and give a vibrant hand job!

your hand, and glide its small jelly nubs across your skin—or your lover's body. Surprise your lover with the hand job of his life—he'd never have dreamt your soft jelly fingers could feel so good. Then use your other hand to caress his testicles, or play with his nipples. Now switch off between rubbing his treasure to grazing his nipples. Gaze into his eyes and enjoy him enjoying

you! Later, take your waterproof mitt into the tub—or lay it on a stack of pillows and a towel for an exciting straddle 'n slide ride!

Feather Teasers

Tantalize the senses with a long, soft, airy peacock feather. Close your eyes and take turns with your lover, caressing each other's tender bodies. Glide it all around, from behind the ear, all the way to your lover's toes. Enjoy the sweet, ticklish, sensual feelings you can only get from feather stimulation.

Playful Submissiveness

Are you adventurous enough to try blindfolds, fur-lined wrist ties and ankle restraints? If you enjoy the interplay of power or submission, there are many toys for you and your lover—as long as you both have a deep level of trust, solid communication skills and a "safe signal" to stop or pause any activity. ♥

Toygasms!

13 Be Safe— Be Clean

You've certainly heard the message—practice safer sex. But do you?

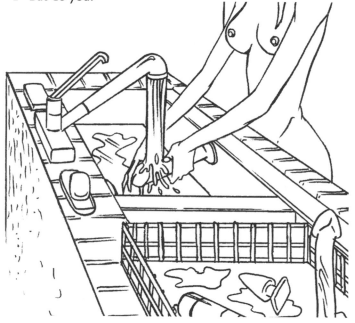

When you practice safer sex, you act in a way that decreases the chance of contracting or transmitting sexually transmitted diseases (STDs), and becoming pregnant. According to the National Institutes of Health:

♥ *Know your partner.* Other than abstinence, a monogamous sexual relationship with an individual known to be free of any STD presents the least risk.

♥ *Wear latex condoms properly.* Use them for vaginal, anal and oral intercourse. And lube them with latex-approved lubricants only. Or try sexual activities that do not involve intercourse.

♥ *Store condoms correctly.* Always have them on-hand if the chance exists for spontaneous sex. And use a new one for each sexual act.

♥ *Stay sober.* Alcohol or drugs may impair judgment, communication and the coordination to properly use condoms.

If you experience an allergic reaction to latex condoms or nonoxynol-9 (an ingredient in spermicides and on many popular condoms), other options may be available. Talk to your doctor or pharmacist, but do not use condoms made of lambskin, since they do not block the transmission of disease.

For more information on safer sex, visit the National Institutes of Health website: *http://www.nih.gov*

Condom Wraps

If you want to share your toys between partners, or even between your own orifices, you can pre-wrap them in condoms. Before you begin, just slip a condom or three over the toy, and peel one off each time you find a new place to put it. Of course, the safest approach is not to share adult toys, but to each have your own to play with! And remember: Never insert anything into your vagina that's been used anally, until you thoroughly clean the toy.

Dental Dams

For the best oral sex protection, dental dams are the best solution. They're simple squares of latex sheets that fit your mouth and act as a barrier to secretions during cunnilingus (vaginal oral sex) or analingus (anal oral sex). They're available in a wide spectrum of fun colors. Before use, rinse with warm water, towel dry, and check for holes by holding it up to the light. Because it's made of latex, use only water-based lube on the dam, as well as on the vagina or anus to amplify the stimulation. Some dams now come with adhesive strips to hold them in place while your fingers do the walking. A dam will not feel the same as a tongue, but it does feel good. Remember, use a dental dam only once.

Latex Gloves

Slip into a pair of latex gloves, and with a snap, you're ready for new explorations! Keep a package of latex gloves handy for anal sex play, or try finger cots—slender latex sleeves that each cover a single finger. They enhance protection against the spread of germs, but even better, create a slipperier surface that will get you where you're going with greater gusto.

Toy Sanitizers

Removing sticky lube and bodily juices from toys are not what America's soap companies tend to boast about. Yet, the problem remains. Now there are cleaning products that get the job done, especially if you've been playing in silicone-based lubes. Take a tube into the shower with you!

Be Clean. Be Safe. Be Healthy

Just follow these simple rules of hygiene so you can be free to concentrate 100 percent on pleasure.

♥ *Wash up.* If you take out the trash and pet the dog on the way to the bedroom, a quick pit stop to lather up with hot water will keep your partner very happy…and healthy.

♥ *Examine your toys.* Check all toys carefully for sharp edges that can hurt, or splits that can hide bacteria. Sex toys have a lifespan, and even if you've grown fond of a particular toy, be sure to replace old faithful when it wears out. And if you improvise your toys, double check that they're sturdy and won't break off inside you.

♥ *Memorize this.* Wear a condom. And use it only once.

♥ *Be really anal!* Take extra care with anal toys. Wash yourself well before anal play, use lots of lube, make sure your toy has a flared base or handle, don't back-and-forth into other orifices, be gentle, follow the natural curve of the rectum, never insert anything sharp, and if you or your partner ever feel any pain, stop and try again some other time when you're more relaxed.

♥ *Clean your toys.* Before and after each use, wipe your toys clean with a cloth moistened with warm water and antibacterial soap or adult toy cleanser. You can sterilize silicone dildos in boiling water or wash them on the top rack in your dishwasher, but do not attempt this with

any latex or battery-operated toys. Dry washed toys completely before storing them.

♥ *Clean your room.* Toss all towels you use for after-sex wash-up right into the laundry, or simply use tissues. Wash all bedsheets after you've sweated them up.

♥ *Keep going and going.* Have a ready supply of extra batteries on hand, so your toy doesn't conk out before you do. If you're not going to be using your toy for awhile, remove the batteries before storing. ♥

Afterplay

Inspired? Aroused? Ready? I hope so, because there's a new world of pleasure waiting for you the moment you find the right toys and techniques for you—and your lover.

So experiment, be creative, cast your inhibitions to the wind. As long as you follow the few, easy to remember safety guidelines here, you've got nothing to lose, and orgasms to gain.

Let me hear from you! Tell me about your toys and joys, your breakthroughs and awakenings, your multiple 'AAHHS' and multiple 'O's—even your letdowns and laments. I'll share your experiences with others who could benefit from them (anonymously), whether it's on my website, or during one of my frequent appearances on radio and television. If I use your technique or idea in my next book, I'll send you an autographed copy, along with a very special toy that'll keep you happy for a long long time!

Write to Sadie at
Tickle Kitty, 3701 Sacramento Street #107,
San Francisco, CA 94118 USA

About
the
Author

As a tireless advocate of women's sexuality, Sadie Allison has connected with millions through PLAYBOY TV, the Discovery Health Channel, Dr. Drew and Adam Carolla's Loveline, as well as numerous other national radio and television programs. While working in the fast-paced, high-tech environment of Silicon Valley, Sadie often advised her friends on their sex lives, and realized there was an educational void in women's sexuality issues. This led to publication of her first book, *Tickle Your Fancy*, which has gone on to become a bestseller.

Now a sex educator for a new generation, Sadie is determined to continue spreading her knowledge of sexual exploration and pleasure, so everyone can enjoy the best sex they've ever experienced.

Photo: Richard G. Martinez

Bibliography

Good Vibrations:
The New Complete Guide to Vibrators
by Joani Blank,
with Ann Whidden
Down There Press, 2000

Anal Pleasure & Health:
A Guide for Men and Women
by Jack Morin, PhD
Down There Press, 1986

Masturbation:
The Art of Self Enjoyment
by J.L. Kulliger
Media Press, 1992

Pucker Up:
A Hands-on Guide to Ecstatic Sex
by Tristan Taormino
HarperCollins, 2001

Sex Toy Tricks
by Jay Wiseman
Greenery Press, 1996

The Good Vibrations Guide:
The G-spot
by Cathy Winks
Down There Press, 1998

The Guide to Getting It On!
by Paul Joannides
Goofy Foot Press, 1999

The Kinsey Institute
New Report on Sex
by June M. Reinisch, Ph.D.,
with Ruth Beasley, M.L.S.
St. Martin's Press, 1990

The Mother's Guide to Sex:
Enjoying Your Sexuality through
All Stages of Motherhood
by Anne Semans
and Cathy Winks
Three Rivers Press, 2001

The New Good Vibrations
Guide to Sex
by Cathy Winks
and Anne Semans
Cleis Press, 1997

The Ultimate Guide to
Anal Sex for Women
by Tristan Taormino
Cleis Press, 1998

Sex for One
The Joy of Selfloving
by Betty Dodson, Ph.D.
Three Rivers Press, 1996

The Good Girl's Guide
to Bad Girl Sex
by Barbara Keesling, Ph.D.
M. Evans and Company, 2001

Special Thanks

Thank you thank you thank you to all my family, friends and associates who have supported and inspired me throughout this adventure in publishing. It's your love, faith and encouragement that keep me going.

To the professionals who helped me create such a beautiful, helpful guide, I am so proud to have you on the Tickle Kitty team: Richard Martinez, Steven Lee, Rich Lippman, John McCoy and Joe Azar. You are truly talented stars. And thank you to the sex toy gurus who generously offered their knowledge and techniques that helped make this book complete: especially Bo Pezzullo and Jennifer Jolicoeur.

And to all the sex toy manufacturers, distributors and retailers--from the growing companies to the grandfathers of them all--thank you for making it possible for all of us to enjoy new and exciting sexual adventures.

Let's click together

The lube requested
by most penises!

Au Naturel ™   Strawberry Lust ™

Water-based. Condom-safe. Stain-free.